Marriages and Deaths
in the
Newspapers
of
Frederick and Montgomery Counties Maryland

1820-1830

F. Edward Wright

HERITAGE BOOKS
2007

HERITAGE BOOKS

AN IMPRINT OF HERITAGE BOOKS, INC.

Books, CDs, and more—Worldwide

For our listing of thousands of titles see our website
at
www.HeritageBooks.com

Published 2007 by
HERITAGE BOOKS, INC.
Publishing Division
65 East Main Street
Westminster, Maryland 21157-5026

International Standard Book Number: 978-1-58549-100-1

This is a compilation of items announcing marriages and deaths
from newspapers of Frederick and Montgomery counties. Abstracts of
chancery court notices have been included when they revealed
family relationships. Chancery court notices were advertised in
those instances when one of the parties lived outside the state of
Maryland.

The newspapers of Frederick account for most of the available
issues of the two counties. Fortunately the Frederick weeklies oft
times carried notices of marriages and obituaries of persons of
Montgomery County. The Frederick-Town Herald was established in
1802 and continued to 1861. The Republican Gazette ran from
1792 to 1826. The Examiner lasted from 1813 to 1913. The New
Citizen introduced its first issue in 1821 when it was named
Republican Citizen and State Advertiser.

Overshadowed by the newspapers of Frederick to the north and
those of Georgetown and the Federal City of Washington to the south,
Montgomery did not introduce a weekly of its own until 1820. The
American and Farmers Register was established in Rockville in 1820,
but the earliest issue known to be in existence is dated 1824. This
paper eventually merged with another Rockville weekly, Maryland
Journal (established in 1825), to form the Maryland Journal and
True American.

Each issue is arranged in numerical order. The index is keyed
to this issue number. Trigraphs at the beginning of each issue
indicate the name of the weekly and the location of copies (originals
or microfilm).

FHB - Frederick-Town Herald on microfilm at George Peabody Library,
      Baltimore and the Maryland Historical Society, Baltimore.
RGM - The Republican Gazette at the Maryland Historical Society,
      Baltimore
PEM - The Examiner at the Maryland Historical Society, Baltimore.
NCM - The Republican Citizen (New Citizen) at the Maryland Histor-
      ical Society, Baltimore.
TFL - True American & Farmers Register at the Library of Congress.
MJL - The Maryland Journal/The Maryland Journal and True American
      at the Library of Congress.

                   Abbreviations used

        co   - county   m   - married
        col. - colonel   res - residence, resides
        Fred - Frederick   ult - ultimo (last month)
        inst - instant (this month)   yrs - years
        Mont - Montgomery

Comments and suggestions are welcome.

                              F. Edward Wright

1. FHB Jan 8 1820/Peter Mathias offers reward for apprentice to saddler's bus. named Josiah Walker, about 17 yrs of age, about 5 ft

2. FHB Jan 22 1820/Married Tues evening last by Rev P. Davidson, George W. Gist to Miss Ann C. Graff, dau of Sebastian Graff, esqr. all of Fred Co/Died 9th inst. at his res in Ontario Co, New York Valentine Brother, Esq. a representative in the assembly from that co and formerly a res of this town

3. FHB Jan 29 1820/Married Tues evening by Rev John Armstrong, John Sprigg of Mont Co, to Miss Mary Dorsey, of Fred Co

4. FHB Feb 5 1820/Died Monday last in the 67th year of her age, Mrs. Susannah Thomas, of this vicinity. She sustained a lingering illness

5. FHB Feb 12 1820/Died at Balt on 4th inst. after a severe illness, Mrs. Catharine Foltz, formerly of this place, widow of the late William Foltz, in the 31st year of her age

6. FHB Feb 19 1820/Died at his res on Sam's creek 11th inst., after an illness of two days, Peter Saum, in the 77th year of his age; remains interred on his farm; Rev Nelson delivered discourse/Died suddenly Tues morning last, Mr. Elie Ogle, a young man, leaving an aged mother and numerous friends /Chancery case - John Harriott vs William Galt and Ann his wife, Joseph Bently (of Eli) and Lucinda his wife, Joseph Taney, junr and Harriott his wife, Henry Spalding and Mariah his wife, Daniel B. Hughes and Elizabeth Hughes. Object of bill is to obtain decree to have deed recorded. The bill states that John Hughes in 1819 made and executed a deed to John Harriott but omitted to have deed recorded. John Hughes died leaving following persons his heirs: Ann Galt wife of William Galt, Lucinda Bentley wife of Joseph Bentley of Elie, Harriot Taney wife of Joseph Taney, junr., Mariah Spalding wife of Henry Spalding, Daniel B. Hughes. Elizabeth Hughes widow of said John Hughes, decd, Joseph Bently of Eli and Lucinda his wife res out of this state

7. FHB Feb 26 1820/On 28th ult the house of Austin Kellogg in Smithfield, Pa, was destroyed by fire and in it his wife and only child, about 5 weeks old. Mrs. Kellogg was hatchelling flax near the hearth, when a coal snapped from the chimney and set the flax on fire

8. FHB Mar 11 1820/Died Tues last in the 43d year of her age, Mrs. Barbara Steiner, consort of col. Stephen Steiner of this place, after a lingering illness

9. FHB Apr 1 1820/Married Thurs 23d ult by Rev William Clingan at his res, Benjamin White, Jr., to Miss Rebecca Darby, all of Mont Co/Married Mon evening last by Rev James L. Higgins, Doct. John H. M'Elfresh to Miss Theresia Mantz, dau of Francis Mantz, all of this place/Married Thurs evening last by Rev David F. Schaeffer, John L. Harding, Esq. to Miss Eleanor Mantz, dau of Francis Mantz all of this place

10. FHB Apr 15 1820/Married Thurs 13th inst. by Rev James L. Higgins, Ephraim H. Maynard to Miss Elizabeth Poole, dau of Dennis Poole, all of this

co/Married in Wash City, on 6th inst by Rev Hawley, William Parker, Esq. of the treasury department, to Miss Nancy Colegate, of Fred Co

11   FHB Apr 22 1820/Married Tues 18th inst by Rev Maleve, William Brophy to Miss Barbara Eleanor Whitler, all of this co

12. FHB Apr 29 1820/Married Thurs evening last, by Rev Kehler, Samuel Powell to Miss Maria C. J. Shaffner, both of Middle-Town

13. FHB May 6 1320/Married Thurs evening 27th ult by Rev D.F. Schaeffer, Thomas Burrows to Miss Elizabeth Winter, both of this city/Married Thurs evening last by Rev J. Helfenstein, Leonard Levy to Miss Louisa Hauser, dau of M. Hauser, Esq. all of Frederick/Married same evening by Rev P. Davidson, George Ott of Jacob to Miss Susannah Biggs, dau of late Ben. Biggs, Esq. all of this co

14. FHB May 13 1820/Died Sun last after a lingering indisposition in the 60th year of her age, Mrs. Magdalena Bogen, relict of the late Doct. J.N.A. Bogen, of this place

15. FHB May 27 1820/Married Thurs 18th inst. by Rev P. Davidson, Frederick Delaplane to Miss Frances Jane Haff, both of Fred Co/Married Tues evening last, by same, William H. M'Cannon, esq. to Miss Eleanor G. Cockey, dau of John Cockey, Esq. all of this co/Died Fri 19th of this month, of a lingering disease, Miss Mary C. Murdoch, dau of late George Murdoch, Esq. She was retired and domestic in her habits/Died Wed last, Mrs. Charlotte Cronise, wife of Simon Cronise of this vicinity. She had only attained her 26th year and not many months; her prospects of health and happiness were as flattering as those of most persons. She was attacked with consumption. She left a husband, an only child, and an aged father

16. FHB Jun 3 1820/Died Sat 27th ult., Francis Bungest, native of Germany, aged 103 years

17. FHB Jun 10 1820/Died at Springfield in Fred Co Wed 24th of May last, Col. William Luckett, in the 81st year of his age/Died Mon morning last about 1 o'clock, after a lingering and distressing illness, Mrs. Mary Hopkins, wife of Evan Hopkins, of this town - Examiner/Extract of a letter from a gentleman at Leanard-Town. "Knowing it will be a great consolation to the friends of Mr. Adam Baer to learn, that he has been found. On Thursday last I understood that a man had floated on the beach, about 30 miles below this, and immediately started to inform his friend Mr. Ford of the report.   We then went after him in Mr. Ford's vessel, but before we could arrive at the place, the humane and generous Mr. John Cole had made his coffin ... orders to convey him back to the shore, from whence we brought him to Mr. Ford's mansion house and buried him in a genteel and suitable manner. ... Mr. Baer had left his clothes below Leonard-Town, which made him start for the purpose of getting them. Two young men accompanied him; they got into the Potomac, and there arose a most tremendous storm, which made them sick, and created alarm. Mr. Baer was standing at the helm when the boom gibed and swept him overboard.   He was, as I learn, heard to call for assistance thirty minutes after the accident but no assistance could be afforded him,

manned as the vessel was, besides it was so dark, that the sailors could not see their hands before them."

18. FHB Jun 17 1820/Married Thurs evening last by Rev J. Helfenstein, George Buckey, Esq. to Mrs. Mary Cook, all of Fred Co

19. FHB Jun 24 1820/Died at the res of his mother in Lancaster, Pa, on 14th inst, Doct. Daniel M. Moore, late of Emmitsburg, in the 28th year of his age, leaving a wife and one child

20. FHB Jul 1 1820/Married Tues evening last by Rev David Martin, Valentine Birely, to Miss Charlotte Mantz, dau of Francis Mantz, all of Fred town/Died 5th of May, at Brookville, Indiana, Mrs. Mary Knight, eldest dau of late Henry M'Cleery of this place/Died Tues last after a lingering illness, in the 32d year of his age, John T. Steiner, eldest son of Jacob Steiner, of Frederick

21. FHB Jul 8 1820/Married Thurs 22d June, William C. Emmit, merchant of Murfreesborough, Tenn., and formerly of Frederick, to Miss Rebecca C. Stokes, dau of the Hon. Montfort Stokes, senator in Congress from North Carolina/Died 3d inst in vicinity of Liberty Town, Mrs. Anne Pumphrey, consort of Vachel Pumphrey, in the 48th year of her age, after a lingering illness of more than 2 yrs. She left a husband and relatives

22. FHB Jul 29 1820/ Bellefonte, Pa, July 15. Died on Wed evening last in the jail of this co, the noted David Lewis, in the 30th year of his age. May his death be a warning to all those who are embarked in the same kind of business, and serve as a terror to evil doers.

23. FHB Aug 5 1820/Chancery case - Evan Dorsey vs. William Woods and Nancy Woods his wife, Charles Hammond, John Dorsey and Sarah his wife, Elizabeth Hammond, John Duttero, Hammond Duttero, Rebecca Duttero and George Cumming and Maria Cumming his wife, heirs at law of Charles Hammond, late of Anne Arundel Co, decd. The object of the bill is to obtain decree for conveyance of part of tract called Charles's Lot in Fred Co. Charles Hammond of Anne Arundel Co decd, sold to Basil Dorsey a part of above mentioned tract. Charles Hammond died intestate. George Cumming and Maria Cumming res in state of Del

24. FHB Aug 19 1820/Died at Emmittsburgh, Sat last in the 71st year of her age, Mrs. Catharine Runkel, consort of Rev Mr. Runkel, formerly of this town

25. FHB Sep 2 1820/Murder committed on the wife of William Baker in the vicinity of Lberty-Town, in this co by a young man and woman, property of Mr. Baker. Mrs. Baker being engaged in the stable, in milking an unruly cow, from which the calf had lately been taken, was followed by the two negroes, one of whom plunged a pitch fork into her bowels. Mrs. Baker was far advanced in pregnancy; probably expired immediately. They attempted to make it appear that the cow had killed their mistress. Mr. Baker had gone to Baltimore; the mother of Mr. Baker was at home with some small children, the only white persons on the premises/Died of consumption on 3d ult, Miss Lucinda Fleming, dau of John Fleming, near Woodsborough, aged about 28 yrs

26. FHB Sep 16 1820/Died Sat morning last, after an indisposition of two weeks, Jason Phillips, Esq., citizen of Carroll's Manor, in this co/Died Wed 6th inst, after a short and painful illness, Mrs. Sarah Beatty, consort of Lewis A. Beatty, in the 23d year of her age

27. FHB Sep 23 1820/Died Thurs last, after a lingering illness, Elie Phillips, res of this co, leaving large family/Died Mon last, Joel Marsh of this town, after a short but severe affliction/Died Tues morning, of the consumption, Miss Eleanor Payne, of this town - Examiner.

28. FHB Oct 14 1820/Married 5th inst by Rev Griffin, John Koontz to Miss Margaret Norris/Married same evening by same, Daniel Springer, to Miss Elizabeth Rose, all of this place/Equity case - Samuel Fundenburg by Jacob Cronise, his guardian vs. Thomas Draper and Daniel Fundenburg. The bill is to obtain decree for sale of enough of the land of Walter Fundenburg, decd, which were devised to Daniel Fundenburg, to raise $2666.60 as a provision for Elizabeth Fundenburg, wife of said Walter during her life and at her death to be equally divided among the six children of the said Walter of whom Samuel Fundenburg is entitled to the 1/6 part thereof with interest from the death of said Elizabeth. Daniel Fundenburg resides out of state of Md

29. FHB Oct 21 1820/Married Sun evening last by Rev Schaeffer, William R. Elvin of New Market, to Miss Caroline Bogen, of this town/Died Wed evening last after a short indisposition, Charles Sower, editor of the Star of Federalism; remains interred in Presby Church yard after address by Rev. D. F. Schaeffer

30. FHB Oct 28 1820/Died Wed evening last after a most distressing illness of a few days, Mrs. Elizabeth Norris, wife of Basil Norris of this town

31. FHB Nov 11 1820/Died Tues 7th inst, John Fessler,Senr, in the 61st year of his age

32. FHB Nov 18 1820/Died Tues 7th inst, of a distressing pulmonary disease, James C. Brashear, second son of Doct. Belt Brashear of New Market

33. FHB Nov 25 1820/Married Tues evening last by Rev Charles, M'Ilwaine, Rev John Johns to Miss Juliana E. W. Johnson 2d dau of late Col. Baker Johnson

34. FHB Dec 16 1820/Married Tues evening last by Rev D. F. Shaeffer, Rev Michael Wachter to Miss Maria M. Wiest, of this place

35. FHB Dec 23 1820/Married Thurs 14th inst. by Rev John Garver, John Shriver, son of Edward Shriver, to Miss Juliana Garver, all of this co

36. FHB Jan 6 1821/Died 28th ult. after a severe illness of 8 days, Mrs. Dorcas Bouic, consort of Peter Bouic, of Mont Co, Md. (This should probably read Bowie). She left a husband and children/Died Dec 29 after a most violent and distressing illness, Nicholas Hall, near New Market, Fred Co, in the 64th year of his age, leaving children

4

37. FHB Jan 13 1821/Married Tues evening 26th Dec, by Rev John Grohp,
Reuben Worthington to Miss Rebecca dau of Dr. Jos. S. Smith of Taney-Town
/Married Sat evening last (6 Jan) by Rev Johns, Stuart Gaither to Miss
Margaret Schell, all of this city/Died Wed last, Miss Elizabeth Christian
Potts, dau of late William Potts, Esq., of Fred Co, in the prime of life
/Died at None- such, res of his father, on 6th inst. in the 26th year of his
age, Robert Young, son of Nicholas Young, Esq. of the District of Columbia
/Died at Lower Marlborough, Calvert Co, on 7th inst., Mrs. Jane Taney, wife
of Doct. Octavious C. Taney, of that place/Died Fri morning 5th inst at his
late res in the neighborhood of Liberty, Peter Shriner, in the 62nd year of
his age; interred in the Cath burying ground at that place. He was a native
of Germany; emigrated early in life; and after passing through various
scenes and vicissitudes incident to human nature, he finally settled himself
at the place of his late res where he remained for about 30 yrs.

38. FHB Jan 20 1821/Married Thurs evening 11th inst at Cumberland by Rev J.
C. Clary, Frederick Augustus Schley, esq., attorney at law, of this town to
Miss Francina C. Lynn, dau of captain David Lynn of the former place /Died
Sat last, Mrs. Elizabeth Cromwell, wife of Richard Cromwell of this vicinity
/Died Tues last in the 64th year of his age, Peter Hardt, sen., after an
indisposition of several months. He was a native of Germany, but emigrated
to this county in early life and settled in Frederick. For 36 yrs he was
organist to the German Reformed Congregation and teacher of their school
/Died same day after a lingering illness, Jacob Steiner, in the 27th year of
his age

39. FHB Jan 27 1821/Married Tues evening 16th inst by Rev William Clingan,
Rev Joseph Hawkins Jones to Miss Elizabeth Clagett, 3rd dau of Joseph Clagett, Esq. all of Mont Co/Died Mon last, Michael Allix, in the 94th year of
his age, inhabitant of this town for upwards of 60 yrs. For some yrs past
his infirmities rendered him unfit for active duty/Died Tues last on Carroll's Manor, Mrs. Mary Ann Thomas, in the 63d year of her age

40. FHB Feb 3 1821/Married Thurs evening last by Rev Griffith, Evan Hopkins to Miss Nancy Patterson, both of this city/Another Rev Patriot gone!
Died at his res in Fred Co on the 25th inst, Thomas Hawkins, Esqr in the
74th year of his age, leaving children. He was among the first to volunteer
as a private and shoulder his musket. Examiner

41. FHB Feb 10 1821/Married at Phila on Thurs evening, 1st inst. by Rev
Hurley, Augustus Taney, esq. of George-Town, D. C. to Miss Catharine, dau of
late Thomas Hurley of Phila/Died at Wash City on Tues 30th ult, after an
illness of 10 hrs, Mrs. Catharine Brengle, wife of Lawrence Brengle, Esq.
formerly of this town/Died Sat last, Mrs. Houck, wife of John Houck, of this
town/Died same day, Mrs. Miller, of this place, after a lingering and distressing illness/Died Wed morning last, of a pulmonary affection, Miss
Elizabeth Fleming, dau of late Arthur Fleming. She had just attained her
19th year

42. FHB Feb 17 1821/Died Wed 7th inst after a lingering and most painful
illness, Jesse Matthews of this co, having attained 70 yrs/Died Wed evening,
7th inst, at his res near New Market, Fred Co, of a lingering illness of

more than 5 yrs, Rev John Pitts, for many yrs a minster in the Meth Epis Church, 49 yrs of age, lacking a few days, leaving wife and 6 children

43. FHB Mar 3 1821/Married Thurs evening 22d ult at Wash City, by Rev P. Davidson, Doct. William Fischer of Frederick, to Miss Harriet Gunton of the former place/Married 20th ult by Rev Zockey, William Cookerly to Miss Mary Ann Gibson, all of this co/Married Thurs 22d ult by Rev Schaeffer, Henry Frazier to Miss Elizabeth Morris, dau of James Morris, Esq. of Va

44. FHB Mar 10 1821/Died Fri 2d inst at the res of Rev William Clingan, in Mont Co, Mrs. Rebecca White, consort of Benjamin White of Benj. in the 24th year of her age, leaving husband, a mother and 4 brothers

45. FHB Mar 17 1821/Married Thurs evening last by Rev Jonathan Helfenstein, Capt. C. Lewis of Loudon Co, Va, to Miss Ann M. Hoffman, dau of John Hoffman, esq. of this co

46. FHB Mar 24 1821/Married Tues evening last by Rev J. Helfenstein, Lewis Jordan, of Shanandoah Co, Va, to Miss Elizabeth Genzen, of this city

47. FHB Mar 31 1821/Died on morning of 19th inst, after a lingering illness, Mrs. Elizabeth Dagen, wife of John Dagen, merchant of New-Windsor, leaving husband and 3 children

48. FHB Apr 7 1821/Died on 29th of March, Henry Koontz, aged 94 yrs; came to Fred Co at 22 yrs of age, by trade a blacksmith; purchased a small farm on Pipe creek where he has res 57 yrs; raised 10 children, most of whom he lived to see established with their families in his own neighborhood, on farms he provided for them. Temperate in his habits, his health was good almost without interruption until within a few weeks of his death; his mind and memory sound and clear to the last. He has left 6 surviving children, 110 grand children and more than 135 great grand children, all inhabitants of Fred Co/Died at Alexandria Mon last in the 62nd year of his age, John Winter, Printer, formerly of this place

49. FHB Apr 21 1821/Married Thurs 12th inst by Rev Jonathan Helfenstein, Jonathan Getzendanner to Miss Elizabeth Derr, dau of John Derr, all of this co/Married Sun last by same, Enos Hedge to Miss Catharine School, dau of Christian School, all of this co/Died in this town Sun morning last of a pulmonary complaint, Jonathan W. Dustin, in the 28th year of his age. He was a native of New Hampshire but for the last 6 yrs had been a res of this co; remains interred in the English Presby Church yard when an address was delivered by Rev P. Davidson

50. FHB Apr 28 1821/Died Thurs 19th inst, Jacob Medtart of this town, in the 69th year of his age. He emigrated to this place with his parents, nearly 50 yrs ago; remains interred in the burying ground of the Evangelic Lutheran Church, of which he was a regular member

51. FHB May 5 1821/Married Mon evening last by Rev Johns, Frederick Marckey, to Miss Elizabeth Dill, dau of John Dill, all of this town/Married Tues evening last, by Rev Jonathan Helfenstein, Lewis Remsberg, to Miss Charlotte

Steiner, dau of col. Stephen Steiner, of this place/Died at the res of her
great grand son (Evan Webb) on Little Pipe Creek, on the 22d ult. Mrs. Mary
Meredith, aged 100 yrs, 11 months, 26 days. Remains conveyd to the tomb by
four of her great grand sons. In the year 1799 she buried her husband,
Thomas Meredith at the age of 96 yrs. She had 8 children, 42 of the 2nd
generation, 151 of the 3rd generation, and 41 of the fourth generation,
which can be ascertained. One dau and one son live at such a distance that
their descendants cannot be ascertained. Pol. Examiner/Died Wed night last,
John M. Beatty of this vicinity

52. FHB May 12 1821/Married Tues evening last, Dr. Richard W. Davis to Miss
Sarah Brashear, dau of Doct. Belt Brashear, of New-Market/Married same even-
ing by Rev J. Helfenstein, William Brengle, to Miss Margaret Grove, both of
Fred Co/Married 3d inst., by Mr. Brutie, at Mount St. Mary's Seminary,
George Foreman of Waynesburg, to Miss Jane Radford, 2nd dau of Thomas Rad-
ford of Emmittsburg

53. FHB May 19 1821/Married Thurs evening last (17 inst), by Rev J. Helfenstein, Col. Stephen Steiner to Mrs. Elizabeth Bausman, all of Fred Town/Died
yesterday afternoon, after a lingering and distressing illness, Mrs. Elizabeth Elliott, wife of Rev Elliott of this place. A few yrs since she came a
stranger amongst us, and now she has departed with the regrets of all. She
has left a weeping family - Pol. Examiner, May 16.

54. FHB Mar 2 1822/Died Fri 22d ult after an illness of several months,
Mrs. Catharine Rohr, wife of George Rohr of this place, leaving husband and
one child, a parent, brothers and sisters/Died Mon night last, in the City
of Wash, Hon. William Pinkney, Senator of the U.S. from Md., aged 56

55. FHB Mar 9 1822/Married at Reading, Tues evening, Feb 26, at the res of
late Gen. Swaine, by Rev Henry Muhlenburg, William Ambrose Lloyd, Esq. of
the town of Northumberland, Pa, to Mrs. Elizabeth Swaine, widow of Gen.
Swaine, with a fortune of $50,000!/Died Fri last, William House, in the 90th
year of his age and at his decease believed to be the eldest inhabitant of
Fred Town/Died Tues last in the 63d year of his age, Jacob Brunner/Died Fri
1st inst, John Shaynholtz, officer of the Fred Town Branch Bank, a young man

56. FHB Mar 23 1822/Died Sat last after a long and severe illness, George
Cox, aged 55 yrs, inhabitant of this city/Died same day, Mrs. Wagoner, aged
22 yrs, wife of Upton Wagoner, of this city/Died Sun last at his res in Middletown Valley, in the 66th year of his age, Jacob Staley, of this co

57. FHB Mar 30 1822/Married Tues evening 19th inst by Rev Wm. Armstrong,
William Hempstone to Miss Ann V. Trundle, both of Mont Co/Died Tues evening
last after a severe and protracted illness of several yrs, Mrs. Henrietta
Krug relict of Rev Krug of this town

58. FHB Apr 6 1822/Died Sun 31st March, after a lingering and severe illness, Henry Poole, of this co, in the 58th year of his age, leaving a widow
and extensive family connexion

FREDERICK-TOWN HERALD

59. FHB Apr 13 1822/Married in New Market Sun evening last by Rev James L. Higgins, Joseph Evitt to Miss Margaret Ann Nichols, both of this co/Died Thurs 21st Mar in Lancaster Co, Pa, Rev Jacob Stoll, aged 91 yrs and 5 months, minister of the Dunker Society for nearly 70 yrs past and within the last year has been known to walk 4-5 miles to officiate his society

60. FHB Apr 20 1822/Married Thurs morning last by Rev P. Davidson, Rev Samuel Knox of Balt, to Miss Zeruah M'Cleery of this place

61. FHB Apr 27 1822/Married Tues 16th inst. by Rev William Armstrong, Dr. Samuel Turner of Loudoun co, Va, to Miss Amanda M. Williams, of Mont Co, Md /Married at Balt, 19th inst. by Rev McCain, William Few, late of Balt, to Miss Susan Ritchie, dau of late Wm. Ritchie, Esq. of Fred town, Md - Patriot /Married Thurs last by Rev P. Davidson, Elie Graff to Miss Amanda Biggs, all of this co/Died Fri 19th inst, at Cumberland, in the maturity of manhood, Beale Howard, formerly of this co. The Court and Bar, of Allegany paid a merited tribute to his memory. Citizen.

62. FHB May 4 1822/Married Thurs 25th ult by Rev Schaeffer, John Shipman, to Miss Miranda Fischer, all of this city/Died at his res in this co on Wed 24th of April, of a lingering illness, Upton Hammond, in the 43d year of his age, leaving wife and children/Died Fri 26th Apr, near Emmittsburg, John Heugh, Esq. of Georgetown, D. C.

63. FHB May 11 1822/Died Wed, 1st inst, at his res in Westminster, Dr. George Colegate, physician of Westminster, in the 39th year of his age, leaving wife and 3 infant children

64. FHB May 18 1822/Married Tues at Frederick by Rev Johns, Worthington Johnson, to Miss Mary J. F. Potts, dau of late Richard Potts, Esq.

65. FHB May 25 1822/Died Thurs morning last after an illness of only a few hours, Andrew Thomson, aged 51 years, native of Ireland, and for several yrs past an inhabitant of this city, leaving wife and 9 children; buried in Presby burying ground

66. FHB Jun 8 1822/Died 17th ult at her res on the Merryland Tract, Mrs. Eleanor Thomas, consort of Col. John Thomas, in the 51st year of her age, and in the 32d year of her marriage, a devoted mother and fond wife - Pol. Exam./Died at Washington on Tuesday last, in the 57th year of his age, Lawrence Brengle, Esq. formerly Sheriff, County Surveyor &c. of this co

67. FHB Jun 15 1822/On Sat evening about half past 8 o'clock, John Fullmer of Callowhill st on his way home, near the second turnpike gate on the Germantown road, was struck by lightning. The one horse gig wagon in which he rode, stopped at the Turpike gate. The gatekeeper came out to receive his toll and after some time ascertained that Mr. Fullmer was dead, sitting upright in the gig. His clothes, hair and eye brows were not singed, but on the right side of his forehead was a chocolate colored mark, something in the form of a Z, and this was the only mark discoverable on his body or clothes - Demo. Press.

8

68. FHB Jun 29 1822/Died on the evening of 24th inst, Mrs. Mary Brown, aged about 63 yrs, after a short but severe illness

69. FHB Jul 6 1822/Married Sun evening last by Rev P. Davidson, John D. Smith, to Miss Christina Gomber, dau of John Gomber, all of this city

70. FHB Jul 27 1822/Died Wed 17th inst. Mrs. Lyon, consort of Dr. Isaac Lyon of this place/Died Fri morning 19th inst. after a few days illness, Samuel Phillips in the 81st year of his age, of Middle-Town Valley

71. FHB Aug 3 1822/Married Tues last, by Rev D. F. Schaeffer, William H. Miers of Cahauba Alabama, to Miss Sophia Birely, dau of late Frederick Birely, of this city

72. FHB Aug 17 1822/Died at Liberty Town, on the 31st ult. Miss Eliza Hammond, in the 15th year of her age; also at New Windsor in this co, on the 3d inst., Miss Frances Roberts, aged 16 yrs; they were cousins and had received at a distant female Academy, an education at which place they were constant companions; and but a few weeks have elapsed since they left it together to return to their different homes. Miss Roberts survived Miss Hammond, only 3 days/Died Wed night, after a short illness, Miss Mary Hickson of this city - Citizen./Died Sat 10th inst. at his res in Mont Co, Robert P. Magruder, aged 50 yrs - Rockville True American.

73. FHB Aug 31 1822/Died at his father's res on Wed, 14th inst, Charles C. Thomas, youngest son of Col. John Thomas, of the Merryland Tract, in the 19th year of his age - Examiner.

74. FHB Sep 7 1822/Married Tues last by Rev Johns, Major Daniel Hughes, to Miss Elizabeth Potts, of this place

75. FHB Sep 14 1822/Married Tues evening last, by Rev J. Johns, Thomas J. Grahame, to Miss Caroline Johnson, youngest dau of late Col. Baker Johnson, all of this place/Married Thurs last by Rev P. Davidson, Doct. Lloyd Dorsey, to Miss Rebecca Ann L. Torrance, dau of James Torrance, Esq. all of this co /Died at Taney Town, Fri 6th inst, Doct. Joseph Sim Smith, patriot of '76 and an officer of the revolution/Died Mon last in the 49th year of his age, Henry Getzendanner/Died 28th ult at his res, near New-Market, James Adams, farmer, in the 55th year of his age/Died Sat last, Henry M'Cleery, Jr, of this city

76. FHB Sep 21 1822/Married Tues evening last, by Rev J. Johns, William Johnson, of this co, to Miss Maria Dorsey of Mont co

77. FHB Sep 28 1822/Married 26th inst by Rev Mallave, Stanislaus Knott of Mont Co, to Miss Eliza H. Harding, of the same co/Died Fri 20th inst by a fall from his horse, Daniel Haine, of this city

78. FHB Oct 5 1822/Died yesterday morning at 9 o'clock Rev Francis Mallave, S.J. aged 52 yrs, and for the last 13 yrs, Pastor of the Roman Cath congregation of this town, as also of the adjoining congregations of the co/Died Tues last in the 80th year of his age, John Reynalds, of this co

79. FHB Oct 12 1822/Died Wed morning last, after a short illness, in the 18th year of his age, Henry Reich, son of John Reich, of this city

80. FHB Oct 19 1822/Married at Mount Pleasant Farm, Thurs evening last by Rev James L. Higgins, Anthony Kimmell, Esq. of Balt, to Miss Sidney Ann James, only dau of Major Daniel James of Fred Co/Died Thurs the 10th inst in the vicinity of Creager's-Town, Christopher Schroyock, in the 89th year of his age/Died near Woodsborough, Sun morning last, after a severe illness, Joseph Hedges, Esq., in the 46th year of his age

81. FHB Oct 26 1822/Died Sun morning last, Henry Kountz, Sen., in the 87th year of his age/Died of the prevailing fever, near the Merryland Tract, Fred Co, John Slifer, Sen., aged 79 yrs, 5 months, and 3 days - Examiner./Brig. Gen. John E. Howard, Jr., eldest son of our revolutionary veteran of that name, is no more; he died a few days since at Mercersburg, Pa, of the fatal malady so prevalent at that place. He attended his brother-in-law, the lamented Col. M'Henry, to that fatal spot - Balt. Morn. Chron.

82. FHB Nov 2 1822/Died on the 24th ult at the seat of Richard Caton, Esq. near Balt, Robert Patterson, Esq. of this co, in the 42d year of his age

83. FHB Nov 9 1822/Death of Lieut. Charles T. Stallings of the U.S. navy, having passed throught the perils of the battle, during the last war, fell victim to yellow fever, contracted at Cuba after an exposure of several days to excessive heat and rain without rest. He was a native of Frederick, entered the navy about 12 yrs since, in the capacity of a midshipman/Died 1st inst. at the res of Lloyd Luckett, Esq. on the Potomac, Miss Margaret Brengle, dau of Lawrence Brengle, Esq. decd, late of this city - Examiner.

84. FHB Nov 16 1822/Married by Rev Johnson Tues evening 12th inst. at the res of Mrs. Elizabeth Charlton, Basil Norris, merchant of this city, to Miss Jane Charlton/Married Thurs evening last, by same, Randolph Campbell to Miss Mariam Butterworth, all of Fred Co/Married same evening by Rev Davidson, William T. Davis to Miss Mary Shire, all of Fred Co/Died Tues last in this vicinity, Daniel Miller, aged 78 yrs and 10 months; remains deposited in the Lutheran church yard of this place. For the last 3 yrs Mr. Miller had been confined to his bed.

85. FHB Nov 23 1822/Married Mon evening last, by Rev John Hargrove, Rev Robert Elliott of the City of Washington, late of Frederick, to Elizabeth, dau of late Daniel Lammot, Esq. of Balt/Died Sun morning last in Balt, in the 35th year of his age, William E. Williams, Esq. of Frederick Co, son of the late Gen. Otho H. Williams/Michael Jacobs, living at Hunting creek, on road from Frederick to Cragers-Town, offers reward for Henry Anstone, apprentice to the shoemaking bus., and stone cutting, age 18-19

86. FHB Dec 7 1822/Died 15th inst ult at his res near Woodsborough. Charles Copeland/Died few days ago, in the 59th year of her age, Mrs. Margaret Weigle, eldest dau of Mrs. Susan Swartz, of this town, leaving an only dau; interred in German Reformed Church burying ground; discourse delivered by Rev Vandersloter, from Phila/Death of William G. Krebs. He was educated at Nassau Hall, where he graduated in 1820. In fall of 1821 he entered theo-

logical seminary at Princeton where on 20th inst the thread of his existence was cut - Poulson's Philad. Daily advertiser.

87. FHB Dec 14 1822/Died Thurs morning last, Mrs. Catharine Doll, relict of late Joseph Doll, of this city, after a lingering illness - Citizen.

88. FHB Dec 21 1822/Died Fri 13th inst, Joseph Fleming of this vicinity, leaving a large family, member of the church (no denomination given)/Fire Tues night last consuming dwelling house of Jacob Winebrener, near Woodsborough in this co, Mr. Coe a near neighbor discovered the fire while Mr. Winebrener, his wife, 4 small children and a young woman were sound asleep. The house was lost but furniture saved; no lives were lost

89. FHB Dec 28 1822/Died Sun last, Mrs. Elizabeth Drill, consort of Andrew Drill, of this vicinity, member of Lutheran Church in this town. On the same day and about the same hour, Mrs. Drill, wife of Christian Drill and brother of Andrew Drill, died

90. FHB Jan 4 1823/Married Thurs 26th ult at Friends Meeting house at Bush Creek, Lewis Coale, of Loudon Co, Va, to Miss Susan Russell, dau of 'Thomas Russell, of this co/Married Thurs 26th ult at Graceham by Rev Kluge, Samuel Saylor to Miss Catherine Rodenheiser; and Tues evening last by same at the same place, Cormack Baxter to Mrs. M'Clemments, all of Catoctin Furnace, of this co/Died in Balt on 24th Dec, Mrs. Weise, wife of Doct. Godfrey Weise, formerly of this place/Died Sat last, Alexander Robertson, son of James Robertson of this co; remains interred in the English Presby burying ground /Died in this town last evening at 3 o'clock, Rev James Redmond, aged 47 yrs, for several yrs past Pastor of the Roman Cath congregations of Wash and Allegany counties/Patriot of '76 has fallen! - Died at Georgetown, D.C. Sun last, Col. Elie Williams, of Wash Co, in the 73d year of his age. His death was occasioned by a long and severe bilious disorder contracted on the survey of the Potomac, ordered by the legislatures of Md and Va. He held many public offices - Torch Light.

91. FHB Jan 11 1823/Married 31st ult by Rev Armstrong, Thomas C. Lannan to Miss Sytha Hechman, both of Mont Co/Married 7th inst by same, Thomas Macgill, of Mont Co, to Miss Juliet Ann Caroline Gittings, of Fred Co

92. FHB Jan 18 1823/Married Sun 5th inst by Rev John Macauley, David Bowlus, Esq. to Miss Sophia Beckenbaugh, both of this co/Died Mon 6th inst. at his res on Linganore, Fred Co, Evan Dorsey, after a short illness, aged 60 yrs

93. FHB Feb 8 1823/Married Thurs evening last, by Rev William Armstrong, Nathan Hammond, Jr. to Miss Jemima Ann Beall, dau of Elisha Beall, all of this co/Died at his res in Mont Co, 3d Feb, after a painful illness of 9 days, Abraham Jones, in the 56th year of his age, member of the Md legislature for some yrs; left wife and family of orphan children who were fostered by his paternal hand

94. FHB Mar 1 1823/Married 27th Feb by Rev Greaves, Isaac Hyde to Miss Mary Lambert, all of Fred Co/Fallen, another patriot of '76 - died suddenly Sat

FREDERICK-TOWN HERALD

22d ult at his res on Linganore, Fred Co, Alexius Simms, aged 67 yrs, leaving widow and 7 children

95. FHB Mar 15 1823/Died Mon evening last after a severe and distressing illness of about 10 days, Doctor William Bantz, in the 34th year of his age - Examiner./Died Tues last, Richard Mills, old inhabitant of this city/Died same day after an illness of but a few days, Ignatius Jameson, aged 52 yrs, wealthy and highly respectable inhabitant of this co. He left a large family; remains deposited on Cath Cemetery in this city - Citizen.

96. FHB Mar 29 1823/Died Tues morning 25th inst, after a severe illness of 6 weeks, Mrs. Mary Springer, consort of Wm. Springer, in the 49th year of her age, wife and mother/Died near New-Market, on 19th inst, Mrs. Anna Maria Musater, in the 90th year of her age; and Mrs. Catherine O'Neill, in the 28th year of her age. The latter was grand daughter to and raised by the former

97. FHB Apr 5 1823/Married Thurs evening 27th ult by Rev James L. Higgins, George W. Maynard to Miss Ann Poole, dau of Dennis Poole, Esq. all of Fred Co/Married Tues, 1 Apr, by Rev J. Winter, Samuel F. Simmons of Fred Co, to Miss Sarah P. Whiffing, dau of James Whiffing, Esq. of Anne Arundel Co

98. FHB Apr 12 1823/Married Tues last by Rev D. F. Schaeffer, John Berry to Miss Mary Getzendanner, dau of capt. Jacob Getzendanner of this co/Married at the same time, by same, Henry Getzendanner to Miss Catharine Kemp, also of this co/Died Fri 4th inst, after a short but severe illness, Basil Dorsey, in the 56th year of his age, leaving widow and child and several grand children; remains deposited in the family burying ground - Examiner/Died Sat last, Mrs. Seguin; interred in Cath burying ground; discourse by Rev M'Elroy - Lib.

99. FHB Apr 19 1823/Married at Shepherdstown on Tues evening, 8th inst by Rev Bryan, Lloyd Thomas, Esq. of the Merryland Tract, to Miss Mary R. Brown, dau of James Brown, of the former place/Died 8th inst. Mrs. Barbara Allen, of this co, in 24th year of her age, leaving three children

100. FHB May 10 1823/Married Tues evening 29th ult, by Rev Bryan, Dr. Lewis Shanks, of Bottetourt Co, Va, to Miss Mary C. dau of Col. John Thomas of the Merryland Tract/Married 29th ult by Rev Armstrong, William Ross to Miss Eleanor, youngest dau of late Rev T. Dade/Married Tues night last by Rev P. Davidson, William Smallwood, to Miss Rosana Rollington, all of this city

101. FHB May 17 1823/Married Sun last by Rev John Gruhp, John Linn, to Miss Rebecca Crous, both of this co/Married Mon evening last, at George-Town, by Rev C. P. M'Illwain, Doct. John Thomas of this co, to Miss Catherine Turner, of the former place/Married Tues evening last, at George-Town, by same, Benjamin M. Miller, of this place, to Mrs. Sarah Wylie, of the former place /Married Tues evening last by Rev P. Davidson, Philip Haller of Fred Town to Miss Dorcas Howard, of Fred Co/Died Sun last, after a lingering illness, Mrs. Susannah Stoner, consort of John Stoner, of this vicinity/Died Fri night last at his res, near Woodsborough, Fred Co, in the 84th year of his age, Jacob Wolfe, leaving aged widow - Examiner.

12

102. FHB May 24 1823/Married Tues evening 13th inst. by Rev Ting, Philip Plummer, son of Jesse Plummer of Fred co to Miss Anne Maria Waters, dau of Jacob Waters of Prince George's/Married Tues morning last by Rev Helfenstein, George Leas of Carlisle Pa to Miss Anna Mary Steiner, dau of Jacob Steiner, Esq. of this city/Died after a short and painful illness, Charles H. Warfield, in the 28th year of his age

103. FHB May 31 1823/Died 23d inst, Francis Mantz, aged citizen of this town

104. FHB Jun 14 1823/Married Sun 1 Jun in Fred Town by Rev Jonathan Helfenstein, Robert B. Stevenson to Miss Hannah Shriner, both of this co/Married Thurs evening 12th inst by Rev Johns, Richard H. Marshall, Esq. of Charles Co, to Miss Harriott M. Potts, dau of the late Richard Potts, Esq. of this place

105. FHB Jun 21 1823/Died Sat 14th inst, George Buckey, Esq. of Buckey's-Town, in this co, old citizen

106. FHB Jul 5 1823/Died Thurs morning last, after an illness of a few days, Master Andrew Thomson son of late Andrew Thomson, decd

107. FHB Jul 12 1823/Died at Tammany's Mount, near Williams-Port, Sat evening last, after a few hrs illness, Matthew Vanlear, Esq. in the 68th year of his age - Torch Light.

108. FHB Jul 19 1823/Died Wed morning last, after a short illness, Levi Hughes, old inhabitant of Fred Co

109. FHB Jul 26 1823/Died Sat last, at the house of her mother in this town, Mrs. Sophia Miers, consort of William H. Miers of the Eastern Shore of this state. Twelve months have not elapsed since she was a blooming bride. The disease was sudden.

110. FHB Aug 9 1823/Died Sun last at the age of 90 yrs, 8 months and 13 days, Rev John Adam Laman, of this co, preacher for fifty yrs; lived to see the 4th generation of his offspring

111. FHB Aug 23 1823/Died Tues 12th inst, after a short but severe illness, John Russell, aged 22 yrs

112. FHB Aug 30 1823/Died Wed 20th inst, Major William Cookerly, aged about 45 yrs, leaving wife and 6 children/Died Sat last, in the 51st year of her age, Mrs. Eve Barbara Shriner, relict of late Peter Shriner, of this co

113. FHB Sep 6 1823/Died Sun last of the present prevailing fever, Mrs. Elizabeth Currens in the 29th year of her age, leaving husband and 6 children, mother, several brothers and sisters/Died Sun last, John Shaffer sen. in the 71st year of his age, long a res of Middletown Valley

114. FHB Sep 13 1823/Married Thurs evening, 14th Aug last, by Rev Alexander A. Campbell, Captain Samuel Stone, of Shelbyville, Tenn, to Miss Mary Ann

Chunn, dau of Launcelot Chunn, of Morgan Co, Alabama, formerly of Middletown Valley, Fred Co, Md/Died Sat last at his res near Liberty Town, John Norris, aged 58 yrs/Died Fri evening last of a pulmonary disease, Richard Nokes/Died Thurs morning last in this city, George Creager, esq. formerly sheriff of this co

115. FHB Sep 20 1823/Died Mon last, Mrs. Rutherford, aged inhabitant of this city

116. FHB Sep 27 1823/Died Sun morning last, after a short illness, Christian Borthol, of this city, young man; remains deposited in German Luth burying ground, attended by Capt. M'Pherson's troop of horse of which he was a member, capt. Green's artillery company and the staff officers residing in town - Examiner/Died 21st inst in 18th year of her age, Miss Elizabeth S. Slaymaker, dau of Alexander Slaymaker of this co - Examiner/Died Fri morning last, John Snoufer, res of Fred Co, and of Carrol's manor, aged 42 yrs, 6 months, 4 days, leaving wife and 8 children - Ibid./Died Tues last in 15th year of his age, John Brengle, son of Jacob Brengle of this vicinity/Died Wed last in the 59th year of her age, Mrs. Barbara Wagoner, member of German Reformed Church/Died same day, John Leather, jun.

117. FHB Oct 4 1823/Married Thurs evening last, by Rev J. Helfenstein, David Sprengle to Miss Caroline Ruth, all of this place

118. FHB Oct 11 1823/Thomas Powell, living at Middle-Town, offers reward for apprentice to the blacksmith bus., named David Dorff, about 19 yrs of age, about 5 ft 7 inch

119. FHB Oct 18 1823/Married Thurs evening 9th inst by Rev Wm. Sedwick, Henry Lowe to Miss Ann Dillehay, all of Mont Co, Md

120. FHB Oct 25 1823/Married Tues 14th inst. by Rev Holfenstein, Ezra Doll to Miss Harriot Zealer/Married Sun evening last by Rev Davidson, Peter R. Shaffner to Miss Mary Hart

121. FHB Nov 1 1823/Died 21 Oct at his res in George Town, in 36th year of his life, Augustus Taney, Esq.

122. FHB Nov 8 1823/Married Thurs last by Rev McElroy, William C. Russel to Miss Emma Frances Sequin/Died Wed evening last, aged 81 yrs, William M. Beall, esq., early became a res of Fred Co, for many yrs prior to his death a citizen of this town; in mercantile pursuits; postmaster for Frederick until a few yrs ago

123. FHB Nov 15 1823/Died at the res of his parents in Phila, 5th inst. in the 30th year of his age, Frederick G. Schaeffer, Esq., late editor of the Baltimore Federal Republcian Newspaper

124. FHB Nov 22 1823/Basil Metcalfe, living near Lewis-Town, Fred Co, offers reward for apprentice to the clothier's bus., named William Cooms, about 19 yrs of age, 5 ft 6 inch

125. FHB Dec 6 1823/Died night of 2nd inst, after an illness of 5 weeks, at the res of her father, Thomas C. Shipley, esq., near New Market, Mrs. Rachel Worthington, consort of Rezin H. Worthington, of Balt Co, in the 18th year of her age; she enjoyed the advantages of a finished education. Her disease though severe and protracted, was not of that character to preclude the hope of her ultimate recovery, until a few hrs previous to her dissolution. A few minutes previous to her death, she called on her aunt, the relict of late distinguished minister of the Meth Church, to pray for her. She left parents, husband and other relations/Married Tues evening, 25th ult, by Rev Nevins, William T. Johnson of Fred Co, to Miss Dorothea, 2nd dau of Alexander Mactier, esq. of Balt city

126. FHB Dec 13 1823/Married Sun evening last by Rev Helfenstein, Mr. C. B. Steiner to Miss Rebecca, dau of Doct. L. Weltzheimer/Married Tues evening last, by Rev Johns, Capt John McPherson, Jr. to Miss Frances Johnson, all of this co/Married 4th inst, by Rev Helfenstein, Christian Winebrenner, to Miss Harriot Rice, all of this co/Married 2d inst by Rev Waugh, Ebenezer B. Hebbard, to Miss Christiana S. Simm/Died in Phila on 26th ult of a pulmonary complaint, John L. Cross, printer, son of Lewis Cross of this city/Died Thurs 4th ult, George W. Littlejohn of this city

127. FHB Dec 20 1823/Married at Woodburn Wash Co, Thurs evening last by Rev Lemmon, Horatio M'Pherson, to Miss Mary, youngest dau of Hon. Thomas Buchanan/Died Sat last, James Linsey of Ireland; died in the house of Samuel Merritt of this town, where every attention was paid him - Examiner

128. FHB Dec 27 1823/Married at Hagerstown Tues evening last by Rev Lemmon, Christian G. Conradt, formerly of this city, to Miss Emily Hughes, of the former place/Chancery case - Robert B. Stevenson, John Stevenson and William H. Stevenson, vs Richard Harper, Peter Stevenson, Mary Harper and Richard Harper, Jr. Object of the bill is to obtain decree for sale of mortgaged premises. The bill states that Richard Harper and Margaret Harper his wife were indebted to Robert B. Stevenson. Margaret Harper is dead having left the said Robert B. Stevenson, John Stevenson, William H. Stevenson, Peter Stevenson, Mary Harper and Richard Harper, Jr. her children and heirs at law. Richard Harper Jr. is an infant 2d he and said Mary Harper do not res in Md

129. FHB Jan 3 1824/Married Thurs 18th Dec by Rev James L. Higgins, Rodney Poole, to Miss Elizabeth Hoy, dau of Nicholas Hoy, all of this co/Married Sun 14th inst by Rev Lanson, James M'Creery to Miss Mary Ann Darcus, all of this co

130. FHB Jan 10 1824/Married Tues evening last, by Rev Schaeffer, Rev John Winter, of Virginia [Gerard's Town], to Miss Henrietta M. Emmit, of this city/Married same evening by Rev McElroy, Henry Jamison, to Miss Exile Barrett, of this city/Died suddenly on 16th of last month in Genessee, in the 70th year of her age, Mrs. Mary Cronise, relict of John Cronise, long an inhabitant of this place

131. FHB Jan 17 1824/Died Fri last, Charles Schell, aged inhabitant of Frederick/Died Sat evening last, after a lingering illness, Mrs. Allice

FREDERICK-TOWN HERALD

Reynolds of this vicinity, in the 64th year of her age, member of the church/Died Tues last of a pulmonary complaint, in the 27th year of her age, Mrs. Charlotte Remsberg, wife of Lewis Remsberg, and dau of Col. S. [Stephen according to another newspaper] Steiner of this place, leaving husband and parent

132. FHB Jan 24 1824/Married 13th inst by Rev M'Elroy, Richard Cromwell, to Miss Caroline Boone, all of this co/Married same day by Rev P. Davidson, Henry Cost to Miss Susan Selman, all of this co

133. FHB Jan 31 1824/Married Tues 13th inst by Rev Grier, Doctor Samuel Annan, of Emmitsburg to Miss Mary Jane, eldest dau of John M'Kaleb, Esq. of Taney-Town/Married Tues 20th inst by Rev Greer. Joseph Danner, to Miss Martha Agnew, both of Emmittsburg/Married same day by Rev Hickey at Mount St. Mary's Joseph Baugher, of Emmittsburg, to Miss Julian I. Shorb, dau of John Shorb near same place

134. FHB Feb 7 1824/Married Tues last by Rev M'Elroy, Thomas W. Carr, to Miss Frances Eliza Arnold, both of Liberty-town/Died at her res on Pipe creek, 22 Jan last, Mrs. Hannah Raitt, in the 87th year of her age

135. FHB Feb 14 1824/Married Thurs evening 1st by Rev D. F. Schaeffer, John Haller, to Miss Mary Brown, both of this city/Died at his res near New-Market Thurs, 5th inst, of a short and painful illness, William Scott, in the 71st year of his age. He was a native of Pa, served 5 yrs in the war for independence; for many yrs a contractor for transportation of the U.S. mail; husband and father/Died 8 inst, after an illness of several weeks, Mrs. Matilda Auchincloss. It is within a few months that she settled in this city as a stranger, without friends, to engage in the management of s small female school. Within the short period she gained the confidence and warm attachment of all with whom she had intercourse/Died after a lingering illness, Mrs. Cromwell, wife of John Cromwell of this city/Died 31st ult after a short illness, Henry Graff, aged 72 yrs and 10 months. He was a native of New Jersey and a citizen of this co for the last 50 yrs - Examiner.

136. FHB Mar 6 1824/Died at his seat in Anne Arundel co on 27th ult in the 69th year of his age, Hon. Richard Ridgely. late an assoc judge of the 3rd judicial dist of Md./Died 18th Feb last and in the 61st year of her age, Mrs. Sarah Clingan, consort of Rev William Clingan of Mont Co, of a short and painful illness, member of Bethel Baptist Church of said co, leaving an aged husband and numerous relatons

137. FHB Mar 13 1824/Charles Cunningham found guilty of firing on Mr. Griffith with intent to kill; sentenced to 5 yrs in the penitentiary - Examiner /Died very suddenly Mon morning 1st inst, Samuel Nixdorff, in 79th year of his age - Examiner/Died at 3 o'clock Sun morning, Miss Elizabeth Hedges of this city, in the 16th year of her age, leaving a mother, relict of Andrew Hedges, being an only child. Ibid.

138. FHB Mar 20 1824/Died Tues 9th inst in 50th year of his age, John Myers of this vicinity

16

FREDERICK-TOWN HERALD

139. FHB Apr 3 1824/Married Thurs evening last, by Rev Helfenstein, George Getzendanner to Miss Elizabeth Salmon, all of this city

140. FHB Apr 10 1824/Died Tues night, 30th ult., Upton Lawrence, esq., attorney at law of Hagerstown, in the 45th year of his age; remains deposited in the family vault with masonic honors; discourse delivered in the German Reformed Church by Rev Lemmon - Md. Herald

141. FHB Apr 17 1824/Died Mon evening last in this town, William Ritchie, of Wm. aged about 44 yrs

142. FHB Apr 24 1824/Died 10th inst., at Hyatts-Town, Mrs. Teresea R. Richardson consort of Samuel P. Richardson of Mont Co of a severe and painful illness/Died Sat evening last in the 31st year of his age, William Stewart; remains interred in Baptist church yard with military honors

143. FHB May 1 1824/Died in this city on the 23d ult, after a short illness, in the 61st year of her age, Mrs. Eleanor Lynn, relict of Col. John Lynn late of Allegany Co/Died Tues 20th ult, Charles Howard of Fred Co, in the 59th year of his age - Reflector

144. FHB May 22 1824/Married Thurs 13th inst, by Rev George Lemmon, Thomas Neill of this co, to Miss Rebecca, eldest dau of Alexander Neill, Esq. of Hagerstown/Died Sat last at the res of his father in this town, William Hauser, in the 36th year of his age

145. FHB May 29 1824/Died 22nd inst. on Carrolls Manor, after a painful illness of ten hrs, Mrs. Mary Hebb, consort of Edward T. Hebb, in the 27th year of her age/Died Mon 24 May 1824 Gen. William H. Winder, in the 49th year of his age - Balt. Amer.

146. FHB Jun 5 1824/Married Thurs 27th ult, at Recess, Elk Ridge, by Rev A. H. Dashiels, Doct. Michael S. Baer, of Balt, to Miss Matilda Chase, youngest dau of late Judge Ridgely/Died yesterday morning, after a lingering illness, in the 74th year of hefr age, Mrs. Charlotte Doll, consort of the late Joseph Doll of this city

147. FHB Jun 19 1824/Died Sun morning, 13th inst., Mrs. Elizabeth Fleming, relict of Samuel Fleming, near Frederick; remains interred in English Presby burial ground/Died in Louisville, Georgia, 27th of last month, after a short though painful illness, of only three days, Miss Catharine Shelman, formerly of this city

148. FHB Jun 26 1824/Married Tues last, by Rev Wiseman, Doct. Thomas Sim to Miss Harriet E. Gibson, all of this co

149. FHB Jul 24 1824/Chancery case - Casper W. Weaver, Erasmus Garrott, John Cost, Tobias Belt and others, vs. Henry Ecard, John Coblentz and Elizabeth his wife, Jacob Coblentz, Peter Coblentz, and Catharine Coblentz. The bill is to obtain sale of piece of land which was devised to Magdalena Buffington by John Ecard, and to apply the proceeds of the sale to pay debts of said John Ecard, decd. The bill states that John Ecard, by his last will, de-

17

vised to Magdalena Buffington, his sister, part of a tract called Maryland Tract, in fee. Magdalena died intestate and left following persons her heirs at law: Henry Ecard, John Coblentz and Elizabeth his wife, Peter Coblentz and Catharine Coblentz, the children of Jacob Coblentz, Barbara Renner the wife of Solomon Renner, Catharine Elizabeth M'Crea, Ann Mary M'Crea, Margaret Jane M'Crea, and James William Thomson M'Crea. John Coblentz and wife, Jacob Coblentz, Peter Coblentz, and Catharine Coblentz reside in state of Ohio

150. FHB Aug 7 1824/Died Sun last, Mr. J. B. Charles, professor of dancing. he had resided in Frederick a few months only, during which he acquired the esteem of those with whom he became acquainted. He was interred in Roman Cath burying ground/William Brookeover cautions that his wife Elizabeth has left his bed and board and taken his children with her, without any just proocation

151. FHB Aug 21 1824/Died Thurs evening last, at Belle Air, res of the decd, Major Robert G. M'Pherson, in the 37th year of his age/Died 9th inst, in the 15th year of her age, Miss Margaret Tice; remains interred in Presby burial ground - Reservoir.

152. FHB Aug 28 1824/Died Mon evening, 16th inst., at his res in Lower Merion Township, Mont Co, Charles Thomson, Esq., in the 95th year of his age, secretary of the Revolutionary Congress - National Gaz.

153. FHB Sep 4 1824/Died Fri morning 27th ult, of a consumption, after a long and painful illness, at the res of his father, Wilson Hoffman, in his 25th year/Died Sat evening the 21st Aug, at his res in this co, Michael Foutz, aged 90 yrs, res of this co upwards of 50 yrs. In his youth he made a profession of religion, in which he steadily persevered until his exit.

154. FHB Sep 11 1824/Died 2d inst. in Balt, of a short but severe illness, Michael Kimmel, in the 42d year of his age, for many yrs a merchant of this city

155. FHB Sep 18 1824/Died Tues last, in this city, after a lingering illness, Frederick Getz, in the 42d year of his age; remains interred with masonic and military honors

156. FHB Sep 25 1824/Married Thurs evening 16th inst., by Rev William Brown, Joshua Daup to Miss Anna Rebecca Brubaker, both of this co/Died Wed 15th inst, at his res near Liberty-Town, after a lingering and protracted illness, Charles Simpson, in the 63d year of his age/Died Sat last at Taney-Town, John Crapster, aged inhabitant of this co/Died Wed night, after a short but painful illness, Robert Ritchie, Esq., editor of the Political Intelligencer or Republican Gazette - Citizen.

157. FHB Oct 2 1824/Married Tues evening last, at Fountain Rock, by Rev Lemmon, William Schley, Esq. of this city, to Miss Ann C. dau of General Samuel Ringgold of Wash Co/Married Sun evening last by Rev Martin, Thomas C. Prince, to Miss Rebecca Geyer, all of this city/Died on morning of 19th inst in Washington, in the 50th year of his age, of the typhus fever, after a

painful and distressing illness, of 16 days, John Crabb, Esq., late Captain
in the U.S. Corps of Marines/Died Wed evening 22 Sep at the res of his
uncle, in Taney-Town, George Rudisel, Junr., in the 25th year of his age.
He came from a distant part of Ohio on a visit to his relations in the
vicinity of this place, but ere he had been long here, death the master of
all, seized him/Died Thurs evening last, after a severe indisposition contracted on his return from the springs, Ninian Pinkney, Esq., clerk of the
Executive Council of Md/Died at Camden, South Carolina, on Mon, 6th ult,
Mrs. Catherine P. Anderson, wife of Doct. Edward Anderson, both formerly of
this place/Died at Locust Grove, the seat of her brother, Benjamin West,
Esq. on the Merryland Tract, Miss Arabella West, in the 53d year of her age

158. FHB Oct 9 1824/Died 2d inst., at the late res of his father, near Frederick-Town, Green Lee Hughes, in the 26th year of his age

159. FHB Oct 16 1824/Married Tues evening last, by Rev Helfenstein, John
Baltzell, of Kentucky, to Miss Charlotte, dau of Doct. Samuel Miller, of
this city/Unexpected death of Rev Patrick Davidson, Sat last, after a short
illness in the 49th year of his age. He was a native of Pa, graduated at
Dickinson College, 27 yrs in the ministry, 15 yrs pastor of the Presby
Church of this city. He left a wife and 8 children/Died Sat last, George
Houck, Jr., of this vicinity, in 17th year of his age

160. FHB Oct 23 1824/Died at his res about 8 miles from Cumberland, morning
of 6th inst., William Hilleary, Esq., aged about 56 yrs, res of that co for
many yrs - Md. Advoc./Died at Cumberland Fri 15th inst, after a short illness, Randolph Campbell, of Frederick Co, aged about 30 yrs

161. FHB Nov 6 1824/Married last evening by Rev McElroy, Henry Simms, to
Miss Margaret Brengle, dau of Nicholas Brengle, all of this co/Died Sat
last, at his res about 3 miles from New-Town (Trap), Frederick co, Michael
Umbaugh, in the 40th year of his age, leaving wife and 2 small children/Died
at his sister's (Mrs. Darcus Cookerly) near this place, Thurs last, 28 ult,
Otho Williams Hughes, son of Levi Hughes, late of Frederick Co, decd/Died
Tues night, after an illness of a few days, John Thomson, son of late Andrew
Thomson, of this city; remains followed to the tombs by relatives, friends,
and members of the warren corps, of which he was an active member - Citizen
/Died Sun 24th ult, in the 15th year of his age, James Lewis Johnson, eldest
son of James Johnson, Esq. of Springfields. Having finished at an unusually
early period his preparatory studies in Frederick Academy, he entered the
Freshman class of the Columbia College at Washington. The first year of his
collegiate course being ended, he returned to spend the vacation with his
friends, and was preparing to rejoin his class, when attacked by the sickness which terminated his life

162. FHB Nov 27 1824/Died Sun morning last, Geo. Littlejohn, long an inhabitant of this city

163. FHB Dec 4 1824/Married Tues evening, 23d ult by Rev John McCauley,
Jacob Sherfeigh to Miss Amelia McNiel, all of this co/Died at Paoli, Il, on
8th inst., Rev William Beauchamp of ths Meth Episc Church, aged about 55

yrs; also on the 16th at Cincinnati, Ohio, Rev Abdeel Coleman, of the same church, in the 42nd year of his age

164. FHB Dec 11 1824/Married Tues last by Rev J. Johns, Henry C. Brish to Miss Eleanor S. Carey, both of Frederick-Town/Married Thurs morning last by Rev J. Helfenstein, Maj. Peter Coblentz, to Mrs. Magdalena Beckbaugh, both of Frederick co/Died Tues morning last, James Murphy of this co, in the 62nd year of his age/Died Thurs last, Miss Matilda Murdoch, eldest dau of Benjamin Murdoch, esq. of this co, leaving aged parent, sisters, brothers/Died Thurs last, Miss Catharine Walling, in the 28th year of her age - Pol. Examiner.

165. FHB Jan 1 1825/Married in Balt on Thurs 23d ult by Rev Dr. Wyatt, John Reynalds, of this co, to Miss Susan B. Winn of Balt

166. FHB Jan 15 1825/Died 5th inst at his res near Sandy Spring, Mont co, Md., Isaac Briggs, aged about 61 yrs, member of Society of Friends, bosom friend of the late Thomas Moore with whom he was laterly also intimately associated in the concerns of public utility in Va and Md. - Nat. Intel. /Married Thurs evening last by Rev D. F. Schaeffer, John Ebert, Esq. to Miss Elizabeth Krug, dau of the late Rev William Krug, all of this town

167. FHB Jan 22 1825/Balt. Fed. Gaz., Jan 14 - Died in our city, suddenly, General Robert Goodloe Harper, about 9 o'clock this morning, after eating breakfast as usual with his family, standing before the fire reading a newspaper. He was 60 yrs of age/Died in Balt on Thurs last, after an illness of 5 days, Henry Shriver, son of Isaac Shriver, of Westminster, Fred Co. He had been attending the medical lectures at the college in this city. His remains were conveyed to the res of his father - Balt. Fed. Gaz.

168. FHB Jan 29 1825/Died at Elkton, Mond evening, 17th inst, Philip Harding, esq., cashier of the Elkton bank (formerly resided in Frederick Co) /Died Wed 19th inst, George Leather, son of Major John Leather, of this co /Died Fri 14th inst, Mrs. Emmaline Nelson, consort of Nathan Nelson of this co. She had been a wife but about 6 weeks when, by an indisposition of a few hrs she was swept from this mortal stage

169. FHB Feb 12 1825/Married Thurs evening last, by Rev Jonathan Helfenstein, John Brish to Miss Eliza Houck, dau of John Houck, all of this co

170. FHB Feb 19 1825/Died Mon last, Mrs. Ann Mary Remsberg, consort of John Remsberg, decd, in the 84th year of her age/Died at Key West, on 12th of last month, Lt. Otho Stallings, of the U.S. Navy/Died 13th inst, in the 59th year of her age, Mrs. Tabitha Pearre, consort of Alexander Pearre of Mont Co, for many yrs afflicted with asthma

171. FHB Feb 26 1825/Died Tues evening last at the res of Beene S. Pigman, Esq. of this city, Mrs. Elizabeth Jordan Shanks, formerly of St. Mary's Co, Md., in the 53d year of her age/Died Fri last, in this city, Mrs. Susan Doll, widow of John Doll, decd/Died Mon last, at the res of David Boyd, Michael Myers, an old citizen of this city/Died Wed last, Daniel Ely, of a

lingering illness; remains interred with military honors by the Frederick Blues of which company he was a member

172. FHB Mar 5 1825/Married Thurs evening last, by Rev Helfenstein, Henry Hanshew, to Miss Catharine S. Stover, all of this city/Married same evening by same, Abraham Nicodemus, to Miss Elizabeth M. Drach, both of this co/Married same evening by Rev Snethen, Samuel Cronise, to Miss Mary Myers, dau of Rudolph Myers of this co/Married same evening by same, Peter Kemp, to Miss Elizabeth Myers, also dau of Mr. R. Myers

173. FHB Mar 12 1825/Breach of marriage contract - Catherine Staley vs Charles Burkhart - verdict for the plaintiff

174. FHB Mar 19 1825/pages missing

175. FHB Mar 26 1825/Married Tues 15th inst by Rev Nicholas Snethen, John Stouffer to Miss Eleanor Stoner, dau of Abraham Stoner, all of this co

176. FHB Apr 2 1825/Died Sat last in the 76th year of her age, Mrs. Lucy Rigney, mother of John Rigney, esq. of this city

177. FHB Apr 9 1825/Married Thurs evening, 31st ult, by Rev Martin, Solomon Lowe to Mrs. Elizabeth O. M'Elfresh, all of Frederick Co/Married Thurs evening last by Rev Shaeffer, David Jackson of Richmond, Va, to Mrs. Mary Robinson, of this city/Died Wed last, after an illness of a few days, Matthias Bartgis, aged about 74 yrs, original proprietor of the printing establishment of the "Republican Gazette," which he guided for 30 yrs. His was the first paper established in Frederick. - Republican Gaz./Died in city of Richmond Sat 26th ult, in the 68th year of his age, William Galt, esq., native of Scotland; emigrated to Virginia in 1775 - he commenced trading with a pedlar's pack and died with an annual revenue of 40,000 pounds. (long obit.) - Richmond Whig

178. FHB Apr 16 1825/Married Sun evening last by Rev Helfenstein, Charles Getzendanner,to Miss Susanna Genizler/Married same day by Rev Martin, Godfrey Koontz to Miss Mary Yeakle, all of this place/Died in Taney Town Fri 8th inst, in the 22nd year of his age, James Riendollar/Died same day, Miss Penda Ebert, dau of John Ebert, Esq., of this place/Died Sun morning last, Mrs. Catharine Thomas, consort of Henry Thomas of this place/Died Sun evening last in the 42d year of his age, William Hane/Died Tues evening last in the 79th year of his age, Jacob Kendal

179. FHB Apr 23 1825/Died Sat last after a lingering illness, John J. M'Cully, Esq., aged 31 yrs; interred with masonic honors in English Presby church yard/Died Tues night in this town, Mrs. Sarah Fleming, widow of the late Arthur Fleming, in the 64th year of her age/Died near Middletown on 5th inst., Conrad Young, aged 97 yrs. In early life, Mr. Young with his wife and several children, emigrated from Germany to this country. He settled in the neighborhood of Catoctin creek, where he remained for about 70 yrs. He was a man of considerable business and wealth. His wife died about 6 months since, after they had lived together in wedlock upwards of 75 yrs. They had 15 children, of whom they raised 11 to the age of manhood, 67 grand chil-

FREDERICK-TOWN HERALD

dren, 99 great grand children, 12 great great grand children. Mr. Young was
the founder and principal supporter of the Luth church at Middletown and
member of that church to the end

180. FHB May 7 1825/Married Thurs 28th ult by Rev Meltzheimer, Robert M.
Beam of Balt Co, to Miss Charlotte Baugher, dau of Fred'k Baugher of Adams
co, Pa/Married Tues last by Rev M'Elroy, Dennis Crough, to Miss Ann Elizabeth Magruder, all of Frederick Co/Died Wed 27th ult, Henry Nelson, of this
co, in the 67th year of his age, native of Montgomery, but for the least 40
yrs, res of Frederick Co/Died Sun evening last, Henry Leatherman, aged 81
yrs, long a res of this city

181. FHB May 14 1825/Married in Phila, Thurs 5th inst, by Rev Ezra Stile
Ely, Lewis W. Glenn, of this city, to Miss Mary Ann Duer, of the former
place/Married Thurs 5th inst, by Rev D. F. Schaeffer, Henry Linton to Miss
Ann Pettingal, all of this co

182. FHB May 21 1825/Married Tues last, at Balt, by Rev Waugh, John Cromwell, to Miss Margaret Sinn, both of this city/Married Tues 11th inst at
Hagerstown by Rev Buchanan, John M. Buchanan, editor of the Cumberland
Advocate, to Miss Mary Grieves, dau of Thomas Grieves, editor of the Md.
Herald/Death of Capt. Henry Steiner Wed evening last, in the 50th year of
his age, leaving wife and 7 infant children. He commanded a company of
artillery, and in 1813 volunteered his services and performed a tour of
duty. In 1814, when the capitol was in flames and the stoutest hearts were
appalled by the dark cloud impending over Baltimore, he again took the field
as a volunteer at the head of his company. In 1815 he was appointed Register of Wills

183. FHB May 28 1825/Married Thurs evening 19th inst, in Taney-Town, by Rev
William Clingan, William Stevenson, of Westminster, to Miss Hetty Teaser, of
Taney-Town/Married Thurs 19th inst by Rev Armstrong, Richard B. Murdoch to
Miss Sarah R. Howard, both of this co/Married Tues evening last by Rev J.
M'elroy, Patrick Tormey, merchant of this place, to Miss Jane Jamison, dau
of late Leonard Jamison [of Carroll's Manor - Citizen]/Died at his res in
London, on 11th of Apr last, in the 77th year of his age, William Murdoch,
American merchant of that city. He was a native of Prince George's Co, Md,
regularly bred to merchandise by Mr. Stephenson of Bladensburg, then a place
of considerable trade. He embarked in business at an early age wtih the
patronage of an elder brother; served in Rev War in a campaign in Pa. At
the close of the war he established himself in London in the Tobacco
business which he conducted eminently to the advantage and accommodation of
his fellow citizens in Md - Examiner

184. FHB Jun 4 1825/Married Tues 24 May last by Rev D. F. Schaeffer, David
Eader, to Miss Elizabeth Toberry, all of this co/Married Sun evening last by
same, Jacob Englebrecht, to Miss Eliza Ramsburg, all of this co/Married Mon
last at Georgetown, D. C., George Stickel, of this city, to Miss Sarah Lex-
ton, of the former place/Married Tues evening 1st by Rev Helfenstein, John
W. Charlton, to Miss Susan, dau of David Kemp, all of this co

22

185. FHB Jun 11 1825/Married 26th ult by Rev Wm. Armstrong, Leonard Hayes to Miss Eliza, eldest dau of John Poole, Esq. all of Mont Co/Died Mon morning, last, after a short illness, Mrs. Louisa Levy, wife of John L. Levy, Esq. of this city

186. FHB Jun 18 1825/Married Thurs last by Rev John M'Elroy, James Power of Frederick Co to Miss Cassandra Harding dau of Elias Harding of Mont Co/N. York Commercial Advertiser, June 13 - Died, Rev John Summerfield, after a painful illness of nearly 4 weeks, native of neighborhood of Manchester, England, in the 27th year of his age and 8th in the ministry

187. FHB Jun 25 1825/Died Mon last, Mrs. Ann Daub, wife of Joshua Daub, of this vicinity; she had been a wife but about 10 months

188. FHB Jul 2 1825/Married at Montauvera(?), Mont Co, 19th ult by Rev William Armstrong, Hon. George Peter to Miss Sarah N. Freeland/Died on morning of 28th ult, Mrs. Sarah Wood, wife of Henry Wood of this co, in the 60th year of her age, wife and parent

189. FHB Jul 9 1825/Died Sun morning last, at the hotel of Mr. Williamson, Mr. N. M. Stephens, a young man whose parents reside in vicinity of Lexington, Ken. He arrived here Fri preceding in the stage, so debilitated as to be unable to pursue his journey. After resting 2 days, his anxiety to reach home was so great, that he determined on Sunday to proceed but death intervened; remined interred in Presby Church yard/Died Sun 3d inst at Washington, Pa, Vachel W. Dorsey, in the 36th year of his age/Died in Beaufort, South Carolina, 22d of May last, after a long and painful indisposition, Rev Mason I. Weems of Dumfries, Va, author of the life of Washington

190. FHB Jul 16 1825/Married Sun last by Rev M'Cauley, Winchester Clingan to Miss Sophia Kolb, all of this co/Died 9 Jun last in Abbeville, South Carolina, Leven Chilton, eldest son of William Chilton, Esq. of Leesburg - Leesburg paper.

191. FHB Jul 23 1825/Died at his res near Middletown, General Joseph Swearingen, soldier of the Rev, during which he was taken prisoner, and endured a long and painful confinement; buried with Masonic honors/Died Sat last after a short illness, Isaac Suman of this town/Died Tues evening, 28 June last, at 9 o'clock, after a serious affliction of about 21 months, James Wagers, in the 64th year of his age; interred in burial ground at Lynganore Chapel; discourse delivered by Rev Reynolds (of Frerderick Circuit). - Examiner

192. FHB Jul 30 1825/Married Thurs evening 21st inst by Rev John Johns, William S. Hatch to Mrs. Mary Spurrier, of this city/Died Sat evening the 23d inst at the house of James A. M'Creary, near Balt, Mrs. Mary Jane Annan, wife of Dr. Samuel Annan, of that city, and dau of Maj. John M'Kaleb of Taney-Town/Died Wed last, Miss Charlotte Mantz, dau of Isaac Mantz, Esq. of this city - Citizen/Died Wed evening, 20th inst, in the 61st year of her age, Mrs. Elizabeth Thomas, relict of Gabriel Thomas, after a few days illness - Citizen.

193. FHB Aug 6 1825/Died at Middletown, Mon 18th ult, after a protracted illness of 4 weeks, John M. Chiseholm, aged 25 yrs/Died near Middle-Town on Thurs 21st ult, Benjamin Routzong, aged about 48 yrs/Died Sun last in this city, David Young, leaving widow and children; interred in Cath burying ground with military honors by Capt. Houck's company, of which he was a member

194. FHB Aug 20 1825/Married Tues morn by Rev Nicholas Snethen, Rev Moses M. Henkle of the Meth Episc Church, to Miss Amelia Fleming, of this city /Married Thurs 4th inst, by Rev J. M'Elroy, Noah A. Shafer to Miss Matilda Brengle, both of this city/Died Sat morning last, Selina Amelia, infant dau of William V. Morgan of this city, aged 11 months

195. FHB Sep 3 1825/Died Thurs morning, Miss Catharine Bentz, dau of George Bentz, of this city, after a severe illness - Citizen

196. FHB Sep 10 1825/Married 1st inst, by Rev Dr. Jennings, John Clemson, Jr. Esqr. of Frederidck Co, to Sophia, dau of late Wm. Price, of Balt Co/In Common Pleas of Lancaster Co, Aug Term, 1825 - Jacob Eshleman and John Werfel, complainants, vs. Elizabeth Miller, late Elizabeth Ferree; Griffith Willet and Mary his wife, late Mary Graff, whose maiden names was Mary Ferree; John Miscimmins, James Miscimmins, William Miscimmins, Israel Miscimmins, Abraham Miscimmins, and John Miscimmins, children and legal representatives of Rachel Miscimmins, decd, late Rachel Ferree; and Andrew Shriver, Abraham Shriver, Isaac Shriver, David Shriver, Jacob Shriver, Adam Forney and Rachel his wife, late Rachael Shriver, John Sekley and Mary his wife, late Mary Shriver, and Samuel Fry and Susanna his wife, late Susanna Shriver, children and legal representatives of Rebecca Shriver, decd, late Rebecca Ferree; David Shriver and Rebecca his wife, David Miscimmins and Rachel his wife, William Miller and Elizabeth his wife and George Graff and Mary his wife - all persons claiming title to tract of land under the will of Abraham Ferree, late of Lancaster Co, decd

197. FHB Sep 17 1825/Died Tues evening last, after a short and severe indisposition, in the 40th year of his age, George Dorff, inhabitant of this city

198. FHB Sep 24 1825/Died Fri night 16th inst, Alfred James, son of Major Anthony Kimmel, aged 21 months, 23 days/Died Sat last at an advanced age, James Pearre, citizen of this co/Died Wed morning last, Miss Christiana Fischer, of this town/Samuel McDade, Fredericktown, offers reward for apprentice to the shoemaking business, named William McVickar, about 14 yrs of age

199. FHB Oct 1 1825/Died Mon 19th ult in city of Balt, William Glenn, late res of this city, in the 21st year of his age

200. FHB Oct 15 1825/Married Tues evening last by Rev Mines, Grafton Hammond, to Miss Mary Elizabeth Ann Rebecca Willson, dau of Thomas Willson, esq. of Rockville, Mont co/Died Sat last, Mrs. Amelia Heinkle, in the 28th year of her age

201. FHB Oct 22 1825/Married in Caroline Co, Va, 14th inst by Rev Cooke, William M. Blackford, Esq. attorney at law, to Miss Mary Berkely Minor, only dau of late Gen. John Minor, all of Fredericksburg/Married Thurs morning last, in city of Balt, Singleton Du Val, Esq. of this city of Miss Eleanor Clagett, dau of of Hezekiah Clagett of the former place/Died Sun last, Jacob Hoff, aged about 70, of this co/Died 18th inst at res of Samuel Hitt, in Wash Co, Md., Rev Daniel Hitt, one of the traveling ministers in the Meth Episc Church, and who has been in the travelling connection upwards of 35 yrs

202. FHB Oct 29 1825/Married 9th inst, Henry Dieterick to Miss Eliza Cronise, dau of Jacob Cronise, all of this co/Married 20th inst by Rev J. Helfenstein, John L. Albert to Miss Mary Ann Stickle, dau of Solomon Stickle, all of this city/Died in Emmitsburg Mon 10th inst, after a short illness, Miss Ann H. Nichols, of that vicinity - Citizen

203. FHB Nov 5 1825/Married Tues evening last by Rev Thomas G. Allen, William J. Dorsey to Miss Susan Rebecca Robertson, both of Mont Co/Married Thurs last by Rev Martin, John Waggoner to Miss Priscilla Gatton, all of this co

204. FHB Nov 12 1825/Died Tues evening last, after a most severe and painful illness, Henry Stowell, of this town, cut off in the prime of life, leaving widow and 3 small children/Died Tues morning last in the 78th year of his age, Robert Johnson, senr., of Middletown Valley, long an inhabitant of this co

205. FHB Nov 19 1825/Died at his res in Liberty-Town Mon evening 14th inst, Major General Robert Cumming, commander of the 2nd division of Maryland Militia, in the 72d year of his age; on Tues his body was borne to the Meth Church

206. FHB Nov 26 1825/Married at Balt Fri evening 18th inst, by Most Rev Archibishop Mareschal, Robert Coleman Brien, of this co, to Ann Elizabeth, dau of Luke Tiernan, Esq. of that city/Married Thurs 17th inst by Rev Michael Wachter, Doct. Henry Kuhn, to Miss Catharine, dau of Major Charles Baltzell, all of this co/Married same day by Rev Martin, John Keedy of Wash Co, to Miss Elizabeth Kenege, dau of Joseph Kenege, of this co

207. FHB Dec 3 1825/Married Sun evening last by Rev D. F. Schaeffer, John Hart to Miss Catharine Herring, all of this city

208. FHB Dec 19 1825/Died at Hagerstown, on 1st inst, at the house of her son, Dr. Frederick Dorsey, Mrs. Lucy Sprigg, widow of late Thomas Sprigg, of Frederick Co, in the 74th year of her age

209. FHB Dec 17 1825/Died 14th inst at the house of John Cromwell, of this place, Miss Charlotte Chenoweth Wilson, dau of Mrs. Henrietta Wilson, of Martinsburg, Va. She was on a visit to her relations, taken sick, and after an illness of only 5 days, marked by severe suffferings, died in the 15th year of her age, an only child, and her mother a widow

210. FHB Dec 31 1825/Married Thurs 22d inst by Rev Mathews, Doctor William Waters, of this place, to Miss Frances Conway, dau of Col. James Hite, of Jefferson co, Va/Died 12th inst at res of her son-in-law, John Getzendanner, Mrs. Elizabeth Hoffman, long resident of this co, having attained 80 yrs /Died in Georgetown, D.C. Tues last, of a pulmonary affection, in the 23d year of his age, David Haller, formerly of this city

211. FHB Jan 7 1826/Died 23d ult, Mrs. Catharine Reitzell, consort of John Reitzell of this vicinity, in the 38th year of her age, leaving husband and a "tender offspring"/Died Wed 28th ult at res of her husband, Mrs. Mary Cockey, consort of Hon. Joshua Cockey, of Frederick Co, one of the senators of the state of Md, after a very painful illness of about 6 weeks, leaving husband, 2 sons and 3 daus - Md. Repub.

212. FHB Jan 14 1826/On Mon 2d inst, Audolph Wilhelm, was run over by a wagon on the public road near Nicholas Whitmore's, about 3 miles from Frederick, and after suffering under the most excruciating pain, died on Fri morning following. His remains interred in German Reformed burial ground; he was a native of Germany, emigrated to this country about 7 yrs ago - Examiner/Died Mon last in the 15th year of her age, Miss Elizabeth Ann Blume, dau of John Blume of this co, leaving father, mother, 5 sisters, 4 brothers and other relations

213. FHB Jan 28 1826/Died Sun night last, Isaac Mantz, Esq. of this place /Died Tues last, John Rollington, aged about 52, for several yrs a res of this place

214. FHB Feb 4 1826/Died Wed evening last, Lewis Green of this city, in the prime of life, leaving wife and 3 little children/Another sage of the Revolution gone! - Died Sun night last, at his res near Westminster, David Shriver, senr, in his 91st year - Citizen

215. FHB Feb 11 1826/Died Sun last, Christian Scholl of this vicinity, husband and parent/Died Mon last, Mrs. Myers, relict of late Christian Myers, in the 81st year of her age

216. FHB Feb 18 1826/Died Thurs last, Alexander McPherson, of this vicinity

217. FHB Mar 4 1826/Married in Georgetown, D.C. Thurs 23d ult, Jacob Markell, Esq. to Miss Rebecca Miller, both of this city

218. FHB Mar 11 1826/Married Tues evening last by Rev Winter, Joshua Motter, of Emmitsburg, to Miss Harriot S. Henkle, dau of John Henkle, of Jefferson Co, Va

219. FHB Mar 18 1826/Married Thurs 9th inst by Rev David Martin, Edward Howard to Miss Ann Buckey, dau of Peter Buckey, all of this vicinity/Died on 1st inst, near this city, after a short illness, Mrs. Mary Cock, wife of Capt. Samuel Cock, in the 63d year of her age/Died at Carlisle on 7th inst in the 24th year of her age, Mrs. Mary Ann Leas, dau of Jacob Steiner of this place, leaving husband and infant dau, a father and mother/Died Sat last, Robert Henderson, aged 52, of this city

220. FHB Mar 25 1826/Died Wed 15th inst, at her res adjoining Carroll's Manor, Mrs. Dorcas Howard, in the 58th year of her age, for upwards of 30 yrs a member of Meth Church; her house was open at times to the preaching of the gospel/Died Tues last 21st inst, at her res on Carroll's Manor, in the 65th year of her age, Mrs. Elizabeth Smith, consort of Capt. John Smith of the Rev army

221. FHB Apr 1 1826/Married Tues 21st inst by Rev Helfenstein, Ezra Houck, to Miss Catharine Bentz, all of this co/Married 7th inst by Rev Wachter, Joseph Becht, to Miss Mary Ann Smith, all of this co/Married Thurs last by same, Peter Angel, to Miss Susanna Krise, all of this co/Married Tues morning last, by Rev John Johns, Rev William Armstrong, to Miss Eliza, dau of Major Roger Johnson, all of this co

222. FHB Apr 8 1826/Married Thurs evening 1st, by Rev Jonathan Helfenstine, Charles Nagle, editor of the Republican Gazette and Political Intelligencer, to Miss Sophia Rollington, all of this city

223. FHB Apr 2 1826/Died Sun last, after an illness of a few days, Daniel McLean, citizen of this town, in the 31st year of his age; interred in Lutheran cemetery with masonic and military honors; discourse delivered by Rev J.N. Hoffman - Examiner/Died Fri last, Gabriel Neighhoff, aged 28 yrs /Died Tues last, Mrs. Hauser, consort of Michael Hauser, esq. at an advanced age

224. FHB May 6 1826/Married at Cumberland Tues evening 25th ult, by Rev N. B. Little, George Tilghman, of Wash Co, to Miss Anna Lynn, dau of Capt. D. Lynn of that place/Married Thurs evening 27th ult by Rev David F. Shaeffer, Levi Mobley to Miss Rebecca Lambrecht, all of this city/Married Sun evening last, by Rev David Martin, George Koontz to Miss Margaret Parks, all of this city

225. FHB May 13 1826/Married in this city Tues evening last by Rev Samuel Helfenstine, Major Thomas Johnson to Miss Catharine Cost, both of this co /Died in the 28th year of her age, Mrs. Patsy Simpson, consort of Bazil Simpson of this co, mother of 3 small children, the youngest not 5 months old

226. FHB May 20 1826/Married Thurs evening 11th inst by Rev John L. Bryan, Andrew Drill to Miss Jane Morrison, dau of James Morrison, Esq. all of this co

227. FHB May 27 1826/Married Thurs evening last by Rev D.F. Schaeffer, Henry Rickets, to Miss Caroline Ortner, all of this city/Married on 16th inst at res of Mrs. Bedinger, near Shepherdstown, Va, Frederick Ellsworth of this city, Miss Susan Peyton, dau of late Daniel Bedinger/Died 17 May at his res, about 5 miles from Frederick, Nicholas Zimmerman, aged 67 yrs, 2 months and 12 days, Paper Maker, which business he followed upwards of 40 yrs, husband and parent; he left a numerous family/Died Mon evening last after a severe illness of more than 2 weeks, William Goldsborough, Esq, leaving widow and family - Examiner

27

228. FHB Jun 10 1826/Married 30th ult, by most Rev Archibishop Mareshal, Francis E. Rozer of Notley Hall, Prince George's Co, Md, to Miss Harriet E. Brooke of Balt, dau of late Richard Brooke, Esq. of this city

229. FHB Jun 17 1826/Died Mon 5th inst, at res of his father, in Frederick co, Captain George Murdoch, late of the U.S. army/Died 9th inst, Miss Fanny Ward, member of the Meth Episc Church, poor in worldly goods, rich in an inheritance from above - Pol. Intel./Died Mon night last, David Mantz, son of Major Peter Mantz, of this city/Died Thurs night 8th inst, George Graff, young man, son of Sebastian Graff of this co

230. FHB Jun 24 1826/Died 12 May last, at his res in Mont co, James Norwood, in the 59th year of his age, husband and father

231. FHB Jul 1 1826/Died Mon evening last, Capt. Samuel Cock, of this co /Died in Winchester on 16 Jun, in the 15th year of his age, after a severe illness of 5 days, Raleigh Colston Thomas, son of the late John Hanson Thomas, of Md - Winchester Gazette

232. FHB Jul 8 1826/Died very suddenly in the harvest field, Thurs evening of last week, Elias Brunner of this vicinity. He was in a remote part of the field from the other hands, shocking grain, and at the hour for supper the family finding he had not returned home, went in search of him and found him lying beside one of the shocks dead. He was 70 yrs of age lacking a few months, healthy and active. He was born and brought up, if we mistake not, and continued to live all his days on the farm on which he died

234. FHB Jul 22 1826/Married Thurs morning last, in the Episc Church by Rev S. Helfenstein, Doct. Robert E. Dorsey to Miss Sarah Ann Duval, dau of Doct. G. Duval, all of this city/Died at Harrisburg, Pa, Mon morning 10th inst, Rev George Lochman, D.D. pastor of the Luth congregations in that neighborhood, in the 53d year of his age, more than 30 of which had been occupied in service of the church/Died at New York, evening of Mon 10th inst, patriot and jurist, Hon. Luther Martin, in the 82d year of his age

235. FHB Aug 5 1826/Died at his res near New-Market, Fri last, William Duvall, in the 77th year of his age - Examiner/Died Sat last in Westminster, Ludwig Wampler, aged 74 yrs, 6 months and 15 days

236. FHB Aug 12 1826/Died Sat last, after a long and protracted illness, Edward Kehler, in the 19th year of his age/Died Sun last, William Springer, old inhabitant of this city/Died same Mrs. Rebecca Poole, consort of Valentine Poole, of this co/Died Mon last, John Hasselbach, Jr., in the 23d year of his age/Died Wed last, James Hilton, in the 35th year of his age/A fatal duel took place on 6 July last, near St. Francisville, in Louisiana, between George Brashier, son of Capt. Ely Brashier of this co, and Theodore Owens of that state. Failing with their encounters with pistols, they encountered each other with swords, when Mr. Brashier received from his antagonist 12 stabs in the neck and breast of which wounds he expired 8 hrs afterwards, in the 25th year of his age. He has resided in St. Francisville for some time, buried in St. Francisville

28

237. FHB Aug 19 1826/Married Wed 10th inst by Rev A. Helfenstein, Benjamin Neidig of this co, to Miss Catharine Snavely of Cumberland Co, Pa

238. FHB Aug 26 1826/Married at Balt, Sun last by Rev Henshaw, Mr. D. H. Bingham of this city, to Miss Ann Bacon, dau of late Dr. Bacon of Balt

239. FHB Sep 2 1826/From Brooksville (Indiana) Repos. - Died at Fort Wayne, 160 miles from this place, James Shriver, chief Engineer of the brigade now in this state (Indiana), for the purpose of making surveys and estimates for canals, apparently of Typhus fever

240. FHB Sep 16 1826/Married Tues morning last, by Rev D. F. Schaeffer, William Small to Miss Maria, dau of Capt. Nicholas Turbutt, all of this place

241. FHB Sep 23 1826/Married Sun evening last by Rev D.F. Schaeffer, Fred'k Gardener, to Miss Catharine Gross, all of this city/Maried Tues morning by Rev John Johns, John A. Donne, to Miss Grace Thomson, all of this city/Died Tues last, Mrs. Ann W. Sprigg, consort of the late Otho Sprigg, of this co, leaving 6 orphan children/Died 15 Aug at her res in Morgan co, Alabama, Mrs. Martha Chunn, consort of Lancelow Chunn, Jr., formerly of Frederick Co, Md, in the 55th year of her age/From Ohio - A young man named Thomas Statton, who said his parents lived in Frederick Co, Md, about 24 yrs of age, had one or two remarkable spots of grey hair on his head, went this morning to help John Jervis to raise a tobacco house and was killed by a log running over him. I believe his father lives near New-Market, Frederick Co, Md. - Mathew Scott, Lion tavern, 28 miles west of Wheeling and 52 east of Zanesville

242. FHB Sep 30 1826/Died Tues last after a short illness, Mrs. Mary Hanshew, consort of John Hanshew of this place/Died Wed last, Mr. M'Bride, superintendant of the turnpike, whose remains were interred with Masonic honors/Died Sun morning last, Justice Kolenburgh, in the 41st year of his age; his illness was short but severe, leaving wife, mother and relatives

243. FHB Oct 7 1826/Died Tues morning last, Benjamin Duval of this co

244. FHB Oct 14 1826/Married Thurs evening last, by Rev Caleb Reynolds, John Porter of Rockville, to Miss Elizabeth Rollington of this city/Died yesterday in this city, of a long illness, which terminated in bilious fever, Miss Mary Sharp, sister of the editor of the Citizen/Died Mon last, Richard Thomas, Esq., of this co/Died Sun last, Henry Berger, of this town, in the 50th year of his age

245. FHB Oct 21 1826/Died Thurs evening last, after an illness of about 3 weeks, Mrs. Rosanna Trisler, wife of George Trisler, merchant of this town /Died 14th inst, Mrs. Maria Elizabeth Baer, in the 75th year of her age - Examiner

246. FHB Oct 28 1826/Died Sat last, 21st inst, at Louvittsville, Loudoun Co, Va, Michael Thompson, merchant of that place, and late of this city, in the

38th year of his age; remains deposited in Cath cemetery of this place.   He
was a native of Athleague, Roscommon Co, Ireland

247. FHB Nov 4 1826/Married Thurs evening, 26th ult, by Rev Nicholas Sne-
then, Doct. E. W. Mobberly to Miss Louisa Mary, youngest dau of Doct. Belt
Brashear, all of New-Market/Married Tues last by Rev J. Helfenstein, Philip
Sneider to Miss Eliza Hull, both of this co

248. FHB Nov 11 1826/Married at Clover Hill, Balt Co, Thurs 2d inst, by Rev
C.Frey, Dr. J. Paul Cockey of Frederick co, to Eliza, eldest dau of John
Kelso, Esq./Died 23d of last month, at her res on Sam's Creek in this co,
Mrs. Margaret Messler, relict of Capt John Messler, in the 65th year of her
age, leaving relations and friends - Exam.

249. FHB Nov 18 1826/Died Wed, in the 70th year, Col. John Ritchie

250. FHB Nov 25 1826/Married at Hagerstown Thurs evening of last week, by
Rev Lemmon, George M. Potts of this city, to Miss Cornelia Ringgold, dau of
General Samuel Ringgold of Wash Co/Married Tues evening last, by Rev John
Johns, Dr. Edward Y. Goldsborough, to Miss Margaret Schley, dau of John
Schley, Esq, all of this city/Married Sat last in George Town, D.C. by Rev
H. Gist, William Sinn, Esq. of Rockville, to Miss Catherine Issabella
Reintzell Locke, of the former place

251. FHB Dec 9 1826/Married Tues 28th ult at Westminster, Levi Davis to Miss
Rebecca Shriver, dau of Isaac Shriver, esq. of that place/Married Tues
morning last, by Rev John Johns, Edward B. McPherson to Miss Ann Talbott,
dau of Joseph Talbott, all of this place/Married Thurs evening last by Rev
J. Helfenstein, Hamilton Jefferson, of Charlestown, Va, to Miss Ann Sophia
Koontz, dau of Henry Koontz, of this place/Married same evening by Rev John
N. Koffman, William Norris to Miss Mahala Naylor, both of this co/Died Wed
evening, 29th ult, in this vicinity, Valentine Buckey, in the 59th year of
his age, leaving widow and numerous relatives

252. FHB Dec 16 1826/Married Tues evening by Rev John Johns, Edward Campbell, to Miss Ann Jennings Johnson of this city/Death of Col. John C. Cockey
of Westminster in this co on Sat morning last, about 3 o'clock, after an
illness of about 3 months; he was about 33 yrs of age and had but just
entered on a public career, one of the representatives from this co in the
last legislature, to which station he was again elected in Oct last; also
elected an elector of the senate of Md in Sep last but was unable from
indisposition to attend. He left a wife and children; buried with Masonic
honors - Examiner

253. FHB Dec 23 1826/Died on 15th inst in 55th year of her age, Mrs. Ann
Ritchie, wife of late Col. John Ritchie, of this vicinity

254. FHB Dec 30 1826/Died at the res of her mother, near Rockville, Mont Co,
on Mon last, Mrs. Martha Wilson, consort of Dr. William M. B. Wilson of
Frederick-Town, in the 25th year of her age, leaving 2 small children one of
whom is about 9 weeks old/Died Fri morning last in the 64th year of his age,
Michael Kalb, long an inhabitant of this city/Died in Liberty town Thurs

morning 21st inst., in the 25th year of her age, Mrs. Matilda Hayes, consort of Joseph Hayes, and dau of Dr. Henry Baker, leaving 3 infant children — Examiner

255. FHB Jan 6 1827/Married Thurs last, by Rev Wachter, at the house of M. E. Bartgis, Esq., Frederick, Henry Haugh to Miss Catherine Linn, both of this co

256. FHB Jan 13 1827/Married Tues last by Rev Reed, David Sherfigh, of Franklin Co, Pa, to Miss Mary, dau of John McNeal, of this co/Died 1st inst, at the res of her son, Mrs. Lucy James, relict of late Daniel James, aged 93 yrs, 1 month, 29 days

257. FHB Jan 27 1827/Died Tues 16th inst at the res of William Wirtenbaker, in New-Market, Lieut. Col. Benjamin Wright, in the 36th year of his age

258. FHB Feb 3 1827/Died 25th ult at his res in Rockville, Col. Upton Beall, about 58 yrs of age, and for upwards of 30 yrs the clerk of Mont Co court leaving wife and 3 daus — Md. Jour.

259. FHB Feb 10 1827/Married Thurs 1st inst by Rev Frederick Stier, Joseph Kemp to Miss Hester Ann R. Day, both of this co/Married Thurs last by same, John Brubacker to Miss Mary P. Fry, also of this co/Married same day by same, Otho Lease to Miss Edith Vanfossen, also of this co/Married Tues last by Rev Jas. Reid, Solomon Sherfy, of Adams co, Pa, to Miss Catharine M'Neil, dau of John M'Neil of this co/Died Thurs last, George Bentz of this place, aged about 60

260. FHB Feb 17 1827/Married Thurs evening last, by Rev D. F. Shaeffer, Lewis Fout to Miss Lydia Ann Routzahn, all of this co/Died Fri 9th inst, Mrs. Mary Simms, consort of Alexius Simms, of this co

261. FHB Feb 24 1827/Married Sun last in Balt, by Rev Waugh, Jacob Carmack to Miss Ann Winnull, all of this city/John Zimmerman living in Emmitsburg, offers reward for apprentice to the tailoring business named Joseph O. Donel, aged about 16 yrs, red hair/Equity case — Surratt D. Warfield, vs. Jeremiah Webb, William Webb, John H. T. Webb and George W. Webb — sale of parcel of ground lately owned by George Webb, decd, ratified

262. FHB Mar 3 1827/Died 20th ult, Jacob Cost, in the 82d year of his age /Died Sat last, Thomas I. Grahame, of this vicinity/Died Wed last, Capt. John R. Corberly of this co [of the U.S. Army — Citizen.]/Died 18th ult, Mrs. Catharine Bowlus, consort of George Bowlus, near Middletown, in the 35th year of her age, leaving two little boys; she was a member of Meth Episc Church for about 15 years

263. FHB Mar 24 1827/Married Tues last at the house of M. E. Bartgis, Esq. by Rev Samuel Helfenstein, Henry Crowl to Miss Sarah Townsend, both of this co/Died Mon last Mrs. Susannah Black of this city at the advanced age of 90

264. FHB Mar 31 1827/Married in Balt Co, Thurs evening 22d inst at Evan I. Crawford's Esq. by Rev Burgess Nelson, Alexander Smith, merchant, of Balt,

to Miss Lydia Murray/Married Tues evening last, by Rev Jonathan Helfenstein, Joseph Fleming to Miss Charlotte Houck, dau of John Houck, all of this vicinity

265. FHB Apr 7 1827/Married 27th ult by Rev Stiers, David Jacob to Miss Margaret Plains, both of this co/Died Sun morning last, Michael Ott, old inhabitant of this city

266. FHB Apr 21 1827/Died Wed last, William Bradford of this city/Died same day of a lingering illness, Mrs. Elizabeth Willis, consort of William Willis, of this city, in the 43d year of her age

267. FHB Apr 28 1827/Died on morning of 22d inst in the 43d year of her age, Mrs. Harriet Brien, wife of John Brien of Cotocton Furnace, and only dau of Col. J. McPherson of this town

268. FHB May 5 1827/Married Thurs last by Rev D. F. Schaefer, Capt Charles H. Burkhart to Miss Elizabeth R. Neighbours, all of this co/Died Tues last, James Morrison of this co, in the 60th year of his age/Died at his res No. 518 Broadway, on the evening of 29th ult, in the 73d year of his age, Hon. Rufus King - N.Y. Com. Adv.

269. FHB May 12 1827/Chancery case - Petition of Robert W. and John B. M'Pherson, grandsons of Samuel Carrick, decd - sale of real property approved/Married Tues last by Rev Martin, Daniel G. Smith of Leesburg, Va, to Miss Eleanor dau of Peter Buckey, of this co/Married same day by Rev D. F. Shaefer, William Hoffman to Miss Hannah Reich dau of John Reich, of this city/Married Thurs 3d inst by Rev D. F. Shaefer, Peter S. Fout to Miss Susanna Thomas, all of this city/Died 4th inst, in this town at the age of 96 yrs, Michael McCann, a revolutionary pensioner, who after living comfortably had saved upward of 100 pounds which he bequeathed to an old friend /Died a few days ago at his res in Middletown Valley, Adam Routzong, of this co, in the 91st year of his age, and had lived with his wife Catharine 65 yrs. She survives him and is now in the 93rd year of her age. They had 12 children, 63 grand children and 55 great grand children/Lancaster Jour. - Died at the public house of Wm. Cooper, Wed night 2d inst. Capt. Isaac Griffith, aged 45 yrs who resided near New-town (Trap) and arrived here (Lancaster) Sat 28th ult on his way home, considerabley indisposed; remains interred in Episc burying ground

270. FHB May 26 1827/Died 17 inst, Mrs. Ann Devitt, wife of David B. Devitt of this city

271. FHB Jun 2 1827/Married Thurs 24th inst by Rev R. S. Greer, James Nichols, esq. of Emmitsburg, to Miss R. A. McGuire, of the former place/Married Tues 22d inst by Rev D.F. Schaeffer, Jacob Young, of Middletown, to Miss Sophia, eldest dau of Jacob Leab, of this city

272. FHB Jun 9 1827/Died Thurs evening last, Frederick Ellsworth of this place who had for some time filled the mathematical department in our academy with much credit to himself, leaving wife and infant dau

273. FHB Jun 16 1827/Died Sat last in Balt, George Getzendanner, esq. surveyor of Frederick Co

274. FHB Jun 30 1827/Died Wed evening last, Samuel B. Leatherwood of this town

275. FHB Jul 7 1827/Married Sat last by Rev Samuel Helfenstein, Samuel Griffith to Miss Maria Foster, all of Harper's Ferry, Va/Died at Taney Town, Md, Tues morning the 26th ult, after a protracted and most painful illness, Miss Lydia Ann Brawner, of functional disease of the liver/Died 6th ult after a protracted illness, Mrs. Sarah Gist, consort of Col. Joshua Gist of this co, in the 74th year of her age, leaving aged husband (the writer is a relation) - Examiner/Died Thurs last at his res in Creager's-town, Maj. Samuel Duvall, of this co, leaving widow, 6 children - Examiner/Died Sun night, after a lingering illness, William Dougherty, printer of this town, leaving a widow - Examiner

276. FHB Jul 14 1827/Died Sat lsat at her res near New-Market, after a severe illness of only three days, Ariana McElfresh, wife of Henry McElfresh, esq. in the 59th year of her age, wife, mother - Examiner/Died at the res of her sister on Merryland Tract, Mon evening, 2d inst., Mrs. Elizabeth Philpott, in the 50th year of her age - Examiner

277. FHB Jul 21 1827/Death of Doct. Robert L. Annan who devoted a great part of his time to experiments in agriculture. His wife died in Feb, 1826, with whom he had spent nearly 40 yrs; he evidently began to sink from that time; he died on the 13th inst, leaving family of children - Examiner

278. FHB Aug 4 1827/Married Thurs 26 ult ult by Rev R. S. Greer, Doct. Jefferson Shields, of Emmitsburg, to Miss Henrietta Grabill, of that vicinity /Married Thurs evening 26 ult by Rev M'Elroy, Michael Crough to Miss Rosanna Conner, all of this city/Died 20th ult in the 50th year of his age, at his res in Mont Co, John Sprigg, leaving 4 orphan children

279. FHB Aug 11 1827/Married Thurs 2d inst by Rev S. Helfenstein, George Hoskins to Miss Mary Ann Kephart, both of this city/Died in this town, yesterday, 7th inst, Rev Maximilian Rautzau, S.J. native of Germany, in the 58th year of his age. He preached in St. John's Church on Sun 5th, had an attack of apoplexy as the Physician thinks, on Monday which terminated fatally on Tues morning at 8 o'clock

280. FHB Aug 18 1827/Died Sat last, at Emmitsburg, after a painful illness of some weeks, Aloysious Elder, in the 70th year of his age

281. FHB Aug 25 1827/Died on 15th inst, William Brashear, eldest son of Capt Ely Brashear, of this co/Died Wed last, John Miller, hatter, of this town /Died same day after a short illness, Miss Elizabeth Cromwell, dau of Mr. Cromwell, of Berkley Co, Va

282. FHB Sep 8 1827/Died Sat morning last, after a short but severe illness, Frederick Markey of this town, in the 31st year of his age, leaving widow and 3 children/Died Jul 27 1827, Eleanor Jane Brooke, dau of Basil

Brooke, aged 4 yrs, 8 months and 8 days; also on 27 Aug same year, Elizabeth
Brooke, consort of Basil Brooke, mother of the dau above mentioned - Examiner

283. FHB Sep 15 1827/Married Thurs 22d ult by Rev Francis Herron, William
Silk to Miss Lucinda Tow, both of Allegany Co, Pa

284. FHB Sep 22 1827/Died Fri last after a lingering illness, Mrs. Catharine Haller, wife of Joseph Haller, of this town/Died same day, Francis
Kleinhart, one of the oldest citizens of this town

285. FHB Sep 29 1827/Married Tues last by Rev William Armstrong, Col. John
H. Simmons to Miss Harriet Beall, both of Frederick Co/Married same day by
Rev Nicholas Zockey, Capt John Matthias to Mrs. Sarah Clemson, all of this
co/Died Sat last, Mrs. Mary Schell, relict of the late Charles Schell, in
the 67th year of her age, one of the oldest members of the Luth Church/Died
Mon last at his res near Liberty-Town, John Campbell, Jr., of this co, in
the 60th year of his age

286. FHB Oct 6 1827/Married Tues last by Rev D. Martin, Alfred L. Moore to
Miss Ann G. Shipley, dau of Thomas C. Shipley, esq. of this co/Died Tues
morning last, Mrs. Shissler of this city, at an advanced age/Died Sun last
in the 40th year of her age, Mrs. Susanna Lare, consort of George Lare, of
this city/Died Mon 24th ult, Christian Fogle, old inhabitant of this co

287. FHB Oct 13 1827/Married at Rockville Tues 2d inst, by rev Thomas G.
Allen, Edward A. Gant, of Frederick Co, to Miss Kitty Ann Anderson, dau of
Dr. James Anderson, of that place/Married at Balt on Thurs morning last by
Rev D. Kurtz, George Trisler, of this city, to Miss Susan Kurtz, of Balt
/Died in this city on Thurs 4 inst, after a short illness, Zebulon Owings,
aged 20 yrs, son of Patrick Owings, esq. of Emmitsburg in this co. He was
educated at the Seminary near Emmitsburg, removed to this place to acquire a
knowledge of the Law - Examiner/Isaac M'Pherson died in his 69th year, last
evening, after a short illness, leaving family of children - Balt. Gazette
/Died in Clarksburg, Mont co, Sun 7 inst., Rev Caleb Reynolds, in the 44th
year of his age, from early life a preacher of the Meth Episc denomination -
True American

288. FHB Oct 20 1827/Died Mon last after a protracted illness of nearly 5
months, James Denning, of Frederick co, in the 65th year of his age, husband, father/Died Tues last, Arthur Fleming, of this vicinity/Died Wed 17
inst at Richlands, the seat of James Cunningham, Mrs. Jane Shaw, relict of
John Shaw, M.D. late of Balt/George W. Falconer, living in New-Market,
offers reward for apprentice to the blacksmith business, named Charles
Thompson, nearly 21 yrs of age, 5 ft 5-6 inch, sandy hair

289. FHB Oct 27 1827/Died Thurs 18th, William Saunders, native of England,
and for several yrs a res of this town/Died at his res in this co, Fri
evening 19th inst, after a protracted illness of more than a year, John
Devilbiss of Casper, in the 78th year of his age; husband and parent

FREDERICK-TOWN HERALD

290. FHB Nov 10 1827/Died Mon last in the 24th year of her age, Mrs. Lydia
Fout, consort of Lewis Fout of this vicinity, dau of Adam Routzong. A few
months ago she was a bride, young, healthy and happy/Married Thurs last by
rev Michael Wachter, Charlton Fleming to Miss Sarah Baker, both of this co

291. FHB Nov 17 1827/Married Tues last by Rev John Johns, Thomas Duckett to
Miss Catharine E. W. Goldsborough, dau of late William Goldsborough, Esq.
all of this city/Died on morning of 15th inst, Miss Rebecca Birely, of this
city, young lady, leaving a widowed mother; a few weeks ago she was confirmed by Bishop Kemp

292. FHB Dec 1 1827/Married 18th ult by Rev Forrest, Joshua Lewis to Mrs.
Ann Chase, all of this co

293. FHB Dec 8 1827/Married Tues evening last by rev Jonathan Helfenstein,
Edward Schley to Miss Margaret Brengle, dau of Capt John Brengle/Died Sun
evening last, Mrs. Susanna Switzer, wife of Jacob Switzer, near Union Bridge
- Examiner

294. FHB Dec 15 1827/Died Sat last at his res, near Frederick, Samuel
Fleming (of Arthur) in the 44th year of his age, leaving wife and 3 small
children

295. FHB Dec 22 1827/Married 29th ult by Rev Matthews, George Beckenbaugh,
esq. of this co, to Miss Martha V. dau of James Ligget, esq of Wash Co/Died
Wed 12 inst, after an illness of 4 days, Mrs. Ann Nidig, consort of Abraham
Nidig, of this co, in the 32d year of her age/Died Tues morning last by Mrs.
Eliza Cockey, consort of John Cockey, Esq., of this co, in the 56th year of
her age - Citizen

296. FHB Dec 29 1827/Died 28th Nov last, at Liberty, in Frederick co, Mrs.
Catharine Sarah Willis, late consort of Henry Willis, and 2nd dau of John
Hambleton, Esq., in the 34th year of her age, leaving husband and 4 young
children, after painful and protracted illness/Died Sun 16 inst, at his res
near Westminster, Joshua Cockey, esq., late a member of the Senate of this
state, for many yrs a member of the house of delegates. He was advanced in
age and in his latter days had many sore afflictions. In the winter of 1826
he was deprived of his aged consort and at the succeeding fall his son, Col.
John C. Cockey was numbered with the dead. - Examiner

297. FHB Jan 5 1828/Married at Balt Thurs evening 27th ult, Howell Few, of
this city, to Miss Eliza Ann Lathan Clarke, of the former place/Married Sun
evening last, by Rev D.F. Shaeffer, William Eagle, to Miss Margaret Fout,
dau of capt. Wm. Fout, of this co

298. FHB Jan 12 1828/Died Sun morning last, after a protracted and painful
illness, Elias Thomas, of this co, in the 30th year of his age/Died at
Annapolis, Tues, 1st inst, after an illness of a few hrs, Jonathan Pinkney,
Esq cashier of the Farmers Bank of Md/Chancery case - Adam Fischer and
Elizabeth Fischer his wife vs Joseph Fogle, Simon Groseman and Elizabeth
Groseman, Robert H. Fogle and others - to obtain decree to sell real estate
of Christian Fogle, decd for benefit of his heirs. The bill states that

35

Christian Fogle died intestate and without issue, leaving a brother named
Joseph Fogle residing, it is supposed, in the state of Ohio, a sister named
Elizabeth Groseman wife of Simon Groseman, both residing in Virginia, the
representatives of a decd brother, Adam Fogle, and the representatives of a
decd sister, Margaret Hill, his heirs at law. Children and representatives
of Adam Fogle (who had previously died) were at time of the death of said
intestate, Christian Fogle: Robert H. Fogle, Joseph Fogle, Jr., John Fogle,
Christian Fogle, M'Keloy Fogle, Rebecca Sullins (wife of Joseph Sullins),
Sally Fogle (now a widow, bearing the name of her last husband, but which
the complainants have been unable to learn) and Nancy Fogle who is unmarried. Diana Edmondson (one of the daus of Adam Fogle) died in the lifetime
of said Christian, leaving children but who are supposed by the bill to have
no interest in said real estate. Children and representatives of Margaret
Hill were in being at the time of the death of said intestate, Christian
Fogle: Christian Hill, Ruth Jenkins wife of Daniel Jenkins, and the complainant Elizabeth Fischer, wife of the other complainant Adam Fischer.
Lewis Hill one of the children of said Margaret Hill, died in the lifetime
of intestate Christian Fogle, leaving two children: Rebecca Randeberg wife
of Philip Randeberg and Martha Hill an unmarried infant. Simon and Elizbeth
Groseman have transferred their interest to one Colin Leach who resides in
Va. Children of said Diana Edmondson, Nancy Fogle, M'Keloy Fogle, Rebecca
Randenburg, and Martha Hill are under age of 21 yrs. Joseph Fogle, Simon
Groseman and Elizabeth his wife, Joseph Sullins and Rebecca Sullins his
wife, Robert H. Fogle, Joseph Fogle, Jr., Christian Fogle, M'Keloy Fogle,
Sally Fogle, Nancy Fogle, the representatives of Diana Edmondson, Christian
Hill, Daniel Jenkins and Ruth Jenkins his wife, Philip Randeburg and Rebecca
Randeburg his wife and said Colin Leach, all reside outside the state of Md

299. FHB Jan 19 1828/Married Tues evening last, by Rev John Johns, James
Grahame, of Calvert Co, to Miss Margaret Johnson, of this vicinity/Died 14th
ult, Mrs. Ann A. M'Kilup, wife of John M'Killup of Taney-Town

300. FHB Jan 26 1828/Died in this city, Sun morning last, 20th inst, George
W. Hubley, Surgeon Dentist, from the city of Lancaster, in 28th year of his
age; remains interred to Luth grave yard of this city/Died Sun evening last,
Adam Keller, aged about 25 yrs/Died Mon last, John Brunner, of this co, aged
about 45 yrs/Equity case - Upton L. Dorsey, Evan Dorsey, William Hobbs and
Susan his wife, and others, vs. Charles Hammond, Nancy Woods, Sarah Dorsey,
Elizabeth Hammond, John Duttero, Hammond Duttero, Rebecca Duttero, Geo. Cum-
mings and Maria his wife and William Hobbs of Samuel. Object of the bill is
to obtain a conveyance from the defendants, except William Hobbs of Samuel,
as the heirs of Charles Hammond, decd, to the complainants as the heirs of
Evan Dorsey, decd, to part of tract called The Resurvey on Charles Lot.
Charles Hammond, decd, in his life time in 1788, sold to Basil Dorsey part
of said tract. Charles Hammond died intestate and defendants except said
William Hobbs of Samuel, are his heirs. Basil Dorsey devised the said land
to Evan Dorsey his son. Evan died intestate and complainants are his heirs.
John Duttero, Hammond Duttero, Rebecca Duttero and George Cummins and Maria
his wife, do not reside in Md

FREDERICK-TOWN HERALD

301. FHB Feb 9 1828/Died 28th ult, after an illness of several months, Most Rev Ambrose Marechal, Cath Archbishop of Balt. He was born in Orleans, France, 1768

302. FHB Mar 1 1828/Died Sun morning last, of pulmonary affection, Miss Margaret P. Thomson, only dau of editor of this paper, having just attained her 22d year

303. FHB Mar 8 1828/Married Thurs evening 28th ult, at Clover Hills, Bush creek, by Rev J. L. Higgins, John Norris to Miss Ann, dau of Henry M'El-fresh, Esq. all of this co/Died in this city Tues morning last, Miss Ann Maria Ringgold, eldest dau of Gen. Samuel Ringgold, of Wash Co/Died 23d ult near Harbaugh's valley, Mrs. Catharine Krise, relict of late John Krise, in the 100th year of her age

304. FHB Mar 15 1828/Died Sat last, George Zeiler of this co/Died Tues morning last, after a lingering illness, Mrs. Elizabeth Getzendanner

305. FHB Mar 22 1828/Died Sat night last, Mrs. Ann Jennings Campbell, consort of Edward Campbell, of this co

306. FHB Mar 29 1828/Married at Balt, on Tues evening last by Rev William Nevins, John M'Pherson Brien, of this co, to Miss Rebecca, dau of Jonathan Meredith, Esq. of that city

307. FHB Apr 5 1828/Died suddenly on Sun morning last, after a few weeks of lingering indisposition, Joseph Smith, long an inhabitant of the co and lately of this city/Died at his res, near Barnesville, Mont Co, Sun last, very suddenly, John Pool, sen., old inhabitant of that co/Died at his res in Washington City, after a tedious confinement, Dr. Wm. Thornton, one of the oldest inhabitants of that city, for many yrs past, presided at the head of the patent office, in the department of state

308. FHB Apr 12 1828/Married Thurs evening last, by Rev J. Helfenstein, Chester Coleman of Hagerstown, to Miss Eliza Graham of this co/Died Sat last, Mrs. Catharine Myers, in the 78th year of her age, for upwards of 60 yrs a res of this place, member of the Luth Church/Died Sat night last, Mrs. Margaret Trisler, in the 87th year of her age

309. FHB Apr 19 1828/Married at Middletown Tues evening, 1st inst, by Rev McCauley, Warren W. Phillips to Miss Catharine P. Creager/Married Thurs evening, 10th inst, by Rev D. F. Schaeffer, Cyrus Nusz to Susan Grove, both of this co/Marred same evening by Rev D. Bossler, Doct. James W. Eichelber-ger to Miss Ann M. Motter, dau of Lewis Motter, esq. of Emmitsburg/Died 8th inst, John Hamilton Hoffman, son of George Hoffman of this co, in the 21st year of his age/Died 11th inst at Balt, Edward C. Pinkney, Esq of the bar of Balt, and late editor of the Marylander/Died Sun last, Mrs. Mima Eader, aged 27 yrs, leaving husband and several children/Died Sun last, very suddenly, Tobias Belt, Esq., of this co/Died Tues morning last, Mrs. Elizabeth Birely of this town/Killed by accident on 24 Oct last, near the town of Franklin, Simpson Co, Kentucky, where he resided, Doc. Roger Johnson Harding (son of Elias Harding of Walter who formerly resided in this co). Doctor Harding in

37

FREDERICK-TOWN HERALD

company with a friend of his, James Davidson Esq. had repaired to the vicinity of Franklin to test their skills in the use of the rifle, by firing at a
target. Mr. Davidson's gun went off and discharged its contents into the
neck of the Doctor, just above the collar bone, completely severing the main
artery, and causing immediate death

310. FHB May 3 1828/Died Fri morning, 25th ult, Joshua Mercer of Anne Arundel Co, in the 47th year of his age, after a protracted illness of 11 weeks,
leaving wife and 4 small children

311. FHB May 10 1828/Died at his res near Buckeys-Town, Ignatius Davis, Esq.
in the 69th year of his age, for several yrs a representative of this co in
the state legislature, member of the Meth Episc Church/Died Fri 2d inst, after an illness of 3 days, Mrs. Rebecca Markell, wife of Jacob Markell, Esq.
of this of this town - Examiner

312. FHB May 17 1828/Married Tues evening 13th inst, at Emmitsburg, by Rev
David Bossler, Daniel Potterfield, of Loudoun Co, Va, to Miss Mary Danner,
of Emmitsburg/Married Thurs 8th inst by Rev R. S. Grier, David Gamble to
Miss Margaret Annan, both of Emmitsburg

313. FHB May 31 1828/Married Thurs 22d inst by Rev James L. Higgins, George
W. Poole to Miss Catharine U. Hoy, dau of Nicholas Hoy, all of this co/Mar-
ried Thurs evening 22d inst, by Rev D. Zollickoffer, David Foutz to Miss
Deborah Norris, all of Frederick Co/Henry Shriner offers reward for apprentice or bound girl named Adalineah Haughn, about 13 yrs of age

314. FHB Jun 7 1828/Married Tues last in the city of Balt, by Rev John G.
Morris, Mr. C. J. Haderman, professor of the French language in the Frederick Academy, to Miss Mary Matilda Norman of this city/Married Tues morning
last, at Georgetown, D.C. by Rev Smith, Francis Lueber, merchant of this
place, to Miss Helen Maria, eldest dau of John Simpson, of the former place
/Married Thurs evening last by Rev D.F. Schaeffer, John Wesley Taylor to
Miss Elizabeth L. Saunders, dau of capt. John Saunders, all of this town

315. FHB Jun 14 1828/Died Fri last, after a few days illness, Col. Ezra
Mantz, of this town; interred in family burying ground

316. FHB Jun 28 1828/Married Tues last by rev John Johns, Clotworthy Bir-
nie, Jr., Esq., attorney at law, of this town, to Miss Harriett A. Worthington, dau of William Worthington of this vicinity

317. FHB Jul 5 1828/Married 22d ult by Rev Helfenstein, William Carlin to
Miss Sarah Lease, dau of George Lease, all of this city

318. FHB Aug 2 1828/Married Sun evening last by Rev Girlling, Robert White
Middleton, of Harpers-Ferry, to Miss Ann Elizabeth Schreiner, of Frederick-
town, Md/Died at the res of Mrs. Barbara Wagers, on Bush Creek, on 14th ult,
Mrs. Ann Wagers, in the 88th year of her age, member of Meth Church, embraced religion at age of 12 yrs

FREDERICK-TOWN HERALD

319. FHB Aug 9 1828/Died Tues morning last, Frederick Riehl, at an advanced age, after a protracted illness, long an inhabitant of this town - Citizen

320. FHB Aug 16 1828/Married 29 Jul at Frankfort, Ky, by Rev Edgar, William Stapleton Johnson, Esq. merchant· of that place, to Miss Rebecca Catharine Miller, youngest dau of Dr. John S. Miller, of Frederick/Died Mon 11 inst, Richard Johnson of Thomas of this co, in the 56th year of his age, ill for past 12 months, member of Episc Church

321. FHB Aug 23 1828/Died 14 inst, John Baer of Hen., in the 42nd year of his age, after a few weeks illness, supposedly from eating cheese/Died on 13th inst, at his res near Middletown, George Bowlus, Sen., aged upwards of 72 yrs, native of Md, he located himself in Middletown Valley when a lad where he resided until his death; member of Luth Church in Middletown

322. FHB Sep 6 1828/Died Thurs 4th inst, Mrs. Francina Cheston Schley, consort of Frederick A. Schley, Esq and dau of Capt. David Lynn, of Allegany Co/Died 23d ult at Staunton, Va, Rev Enoch George, one of the Bishops of the Meth Episc Church, aged about 60 yrs

323. FHB Sep 13 1828/Married Tues 2d inst, in Balt, by Rev Morris, Rev Daniel J. Hauer, of Botetourt Co, Va, to Miss Henrietta Warner of Balt/Died Thurs evening, 4th inst, Miss Elizabeth Leab, dau of Jacob Leab, of this city - Examiner

324. FHB Sep 20 1828/Died Fri evening 12th inst, after a short illness, Thomas A. Baltzell, son of Thomas Baltzell, merchant of Balt, in the 22d year of his age. He was on a visit to his relatives in this place. His system, previously debilitated, suddenly gave way to one of those attacks which could not have been foreseen/Died Thurs last, at an advanced age, Mrs. Mary Baer, relict of John Baer, of this co

325. FHB Sep 27 1828/Died 1st inst, at the res of his mother, near Middletown, Hanson Phillips, aged 16 yrs; found salvation at camp meeting in Wash Co 12 months earlier

326. FHB Oct 11 1828/Died Sat morning last, Mrs. Elizabeth Gebhart, consort of John Gebhart, aged 52 yrs/Died Mon last, Mrs. Mary Bond, in the 61st year of her age/Died same day, Mrs. Rebecca Whittington, aged 53 yrs

327. FHB Oct 25 1828/Married Tues morning last by rev John Johns, Abner Campbell to Miss Catharine Helfenstein, dau of Rev Jonathan Helfenstein/Married Tues evening by same, Dr. Charles W. Johnson to Miss Eleanor M. Tyler, dau of Dr. Wm. Bradley Tyler, all of this city

328. FHB Nov 1 1828/Died Wed morning last, Mrs. Anna Mary Schley, consort of David Schley, Esq of this co, after a few days illness, leaving husband and family of small children/Died 17 inst, at hs res in Lower Marlboro, Calvert Co, Richard Grahame, Esq in the 60th year of his age, leaving wife and 6 children - Balt. paper/Chancery case - Samuel Knox & wife and others, vs. John Knight and others. Object of the bill is to obtain decree for sale of part of Lot 104 in Frederick. The bill states the land, on the death of

Henry M'Cleery, descended to his heirs, that some of them reside out of the state, to wit: John Knight resides in Mississippi, John Hanna and Martha R. Hanna, Thomas J. Knight, Henry W. Knight, Susannah F. Knight and William F. Knight reside in Indiana and Michael M'Clanagan resides in Pa

329. FHB Nov 8 1828/Died Fri 31st ult, Mrs. Catharine Weaver, in the 83d year of her age/Died Fri night, 31st ult, in 64th year of his age, John Morgan of this town/Died Sun last, Mrs. Sophia Brunner, about 83 yrs of age/Mrs. Eleanor Murdoch, relict of George Murdoch, esq of Frederick died 31st ult, in her 81st year

330. FHB Nov 15 1828/Married Tues 4th inst, by Rev Wm. Armstrong, Henry Kemp, son of Col. Henry Kemp, to Miss Amanda Trail, dau of William Trail of Mont Co

331. FHB Nov 22 1828/Married Tues 18th inst at Shrinerea, Frederick co, by Rev M'Elroy, Peter Lugenbeel to Miss Martha E. Lawrence, eldest dau of capt. John S. Lawrence, all of this co/Married at the same time and by same, Evan Dorsey, of Tiffin, Ohio, to Miss Juliana M. Lawrence, 2nd dau of capt. J.S. Lawrence, of this co [John S. Lawrence - Citizen.]

332. FHB Nov 22 1828/Equity case - Nancy Shoemaker and Jacob Shoemaker and others vs Adam Lichtenwalter and others - Object of bill is to obtain decree for sale of real estate of William Ferguson, of Frederick Co, decd who died instesate and without issue in Aug 1821, owning land, 105 acres. His brother and sisters and children of such brothers and sisters as are dead, are his legal heirs. The following named heirs and representatives of William Ferguson, decd, resided in the states hereafter mentioned, and beyond the process of this court: Elizabeth Hodge and Francis her husband, Mary Allen and Robert her husband, Jane Paragraft and Jonathan her husband, Esther Orr and Robert her husband, Martha Elerander and John her husband, Susan Rodges and William her husband, and John Ferguson, all residents in Tennessee; James Anders (widower of Esther Anders, decd) tenant by the courtesy, Samuel Anders, Henry Anders, John Anders, Alexander Anders, Elizabeth Perryman and her husband, Nancy Mayner and Elijah her husband, Margaret Anders, and Esther Anders, all residing in Tennessee; Samuel Ferguson, John Ferguson, William Ferguson, Thomas Ferguson, James Ferguson, Henry Ferguson, Elizabeth Ferguson, Jane Ferguson, Sarah Ferguson, Nancy Ferguson, Hugh Ferguson, and Margaret Ferguson, all residing in the state of Kentucky; Samuel Paxton, William Paxton, Elizabeth M'Comb and William her husband, Sarah Shaw and John her husband, Hannah Moore and John her husband, all residing in Ohio; Margaret Stead and John her husband, Sarah Morrison and Alexander her husband, Esther Ferguson, John Ferguson, Nancy Ferguson, Mary Ferguson, Eliza Ann Ferguson, Jane Ferguson, Elizabeth Urting and Charles her husband, William Ferguson, James Ferguson, Hugh Ferguson, all residing in Ohio; Samuel Ferguson, James Ferguson, Margaret Clabaughand, John her husband, all residents of Tennessee

333. FHB Nov 22 1828/Equity case - William B. Hebbard adm'r of Matilda Harris decd, and others, vs. Abner Magers and Ruth his wife, and others. Object of the bill is to obtain a decree for sale of real estate of John Harris, decd, son to Thomas Harris, decd, for payment of legacies due to

William B. Hebbard, admr of Matilda Harris, decd, and Margaret Harris, and for the payment of certin money due to George C. Harris and Washington Harris, under a valuation of the real estate devised to said John Harris by Thomas Harris his father, made by the executors of said Thomas Harris, decd. The bill states that Thomas Harris, decd, by his will, bequeathed certain legacies therein mentioned to his dau Margaret Harris and to his grand dau Matilda Harris, which are a lien on the real est of said John Harris, decd, and remain unpaid, and ordered his executors to value his four farms devised to his four sons so as to make them equal in value, and that each should pay to the other so much as thus to equalize the value; that John Harris died without having paid to George C. Harris and Washington Harris the sums of money comming to them under said valuation; that John Harris died intestate and without issue; that his brothers and sisters, and the children of such brothers and sisters who are dead, are his heirs at law, of whom the following named do not reside within Md, but in Ohio, to wit, Matilda, a niece to said John Harris, who married Edward Benton, Ruth, a sister to John Harris who married Thomas Sellman

334. FHB Dec 6 1828/Married Tues evening last, by Rev J. Helfenstein, Lawrence J. Brengle, to Miss Catharine C. Shriver, dau of Andrew Shriver, esq. all of this co/Died 7th ult, Mrs. Amelia Smith, wife of Capt. Daniel Smith of this co, in the 66th year of age. Mrs. Smith retired to bed at the usual hour but afterwards was affected with a difficulty of breathing and expired soon thereafter. She had been married 45 yrs, had raised 10 children, and lived to see 33 grand children

335. FHB Dec 13 1828/Died last Sat night, at the res of his son-in-law, Henry Thomas of Gabriel, on Carroll's Manor, George Ger, for many yrs a res of this co/Died Mon morning last, William Michael, innkeeper, of this town, in the 54th year of his age

336. FHB Dec 27 1828/Married Tues last, by Rev D.F. Schaeffer, John Zimmerman (paper maker) to Miss Catharine Straeffer (Schaeffer?), all of this co /Death of Mrs. Darcus Haller, consort of Philip Haller, of this place, and dau of Joseph and Darcus Howard, late of Carroll's Manor, decd, aged 26 yrs, leaving husband and a little dau - Examiner

337. FHB Jan 10 1829/Died Thurs 8th inst, in the 70th year of her age, Mrs. Elizabeth Baer, wife of Henry Baer of this city, after protracted affection of cancer

338. FHB Jan 17 1829/Died Sat morning last, after a long and severe illness, John Buckey, in the 48th year of his age/Died Fri evening 9th inst, Mrs. Magdalen Lambright, in the 51st year of her age/Died Wed morning last, in the 28th year of her age, Mrs. Elizabeth Shope, wife of George B. Shope, of this town; her suffering though of short duration, was of a most excruciating nautre

339. FHB Jan 31 1829/Married Sun 25th inst, by Rev John M'Elwoy, John Moreland to Miss Elizabeth Wilcoxen, all of this co/Died Sat 24th inst, Bazil Brooke, esq. for many yrs a res of this co

340. FHB Feb 7 1829/Married Tues evening last, by Rev Schaeffer, Abraham Blessing, merchant, of Trap-town, to Miss Mary Ent, only dau of Capt G. W. Ent of this town/Married Thurs 22d ult by same, John Kaufman of Carlisle, to Miss Susan Pool dau of Walter Pool, esq of this co/Married Tues 27th by same, Daniel Smelzer, to Miss Margaret Burns, all of this co/Married Thurs evening 29th by same, Leonard S. Grove, to Miss Rebecca Fout dau of Baltzer Fout, of this co/Married Tues evening last, by Rev Jarard Rice, Col. Nelson Luckett, to Miss Elenor McGill, dau of Patrick McGill, Esq. all of this co

341. FHB Feb 14 1828/Married Tues morning last by Rev Armstrong, Doct. George E. Pryor to Miss Caroline Graaff, dau of Sebastian Graaff, all of this co

342. FHB Feb 21 1828/Married Tues 10th inst by Rev Jacob Larkin, James Whitehill to Miss Ann Campbell, both of this co/Married at Balt on 12th inst, by Rev Morrison, Henry Mantz to Miss Sophia, dau of Wm. Branson/Died near Union-Town in this co, 4th inst, of a pulmonary complaint, John D. Norris, son of Jonathan Norris, in the 23d year of his age; interred near new Meth meeting house in Union Town - Citizen

343. FHB Feb 28 1829/Married Tues evening last, by Rev Wachter, Doct. Wilson Kolb of Woodsborough, to Miss Margaret Harman, of this city/Died Wed 18th inst, Patrick Reid, of Emmitsburg, Md/Died wed last, after a protracted illness, Doct. Lewis Creager, of Middletown, in this co

344. FHB Mar 7 1829/Died Fri 27th ult of typhus fever, Allen P. Duvall, printer, aged about 21 yrs, leaving aged and widowed mother/Died Fri last, Miss Cornelia Swearingen, youngest dau of general Joseph Swearingen, late of Frederick co, decd

345. FHB Mar 14 1829/Died morning of Mar 1, Samuel Switzer, 2nd son of Jacob Switzer. He had entered the water house of the mill belonging to his father, on Little Pipe Creek to clear the wheel from ice, and after some time was discovered by his brother, lying between the wheel and fore bay, lifeless, his scull fractured and head bruised, apparently stood on the arm of the wheel and the weight of the ice and water prevented his stopping its motion/Died Tues last, Mrs. Mary Brunner, consort of Jno. Brunner of J. of this town, leaving husband and several small children - Citizen/Died morning of Thurs 26 ult, John Shaw, in the 84th year of his age, of this city, armourer to the state during the Rev war - Md. Gaz.

346. FHB Mar 21 1829/Died in Emmitsburg 12th inst of pulmonary disease, Alexander Jarboe, in the 35th year of his age, leaving wife and 2 infant children - Citizen/Died Mon last, after an illness of a few days, Mrs. Elizabeth Springer, wife of Daniel Springer of this city, leaving husband and 3 small children, and a parent/Married Tues morning, 17th inst by Rev Jonathan Helfenstein, Cornelius Shriner of Ceresville, to Miss Rebecca Scholl, of this co

347. FHB Mar 28 1829/Married Tues 17th inst by Rev M'Cauly, Joseph L. Perkin of Pennsylvania, to Miss Ann Howard of Middletown/Married in Middletown Thurs evening, 19th inst, by same, James Stover to Miss Alice Ann Eliza

Fleming, both of this town/Died at res of William Shepherd, Esq 17th inst,
Mrs. Tamer Hartley, about 70 yrs of age, and for last 40 yrs suffered much
bodily affliction - Examiner/Died same day at his res on Beaver dam, Abraham
Hartman, at an advanced age - Examiner/Died Wed 18th inst at his res near
Little Pipe Creek, Rudolph Switzer, in his 90th year - Examiner

348. FHB Apr 4 1829/Died Sun evening 29 Mar, Mrs. Elizabeth Johnson, consort
of Thomas W. Johnson, in the 32d year of her age, leaving husband and 7
small children

349. FHB Apr 11 1829/Died Sun morning 5th inst, Miss Elizabeth Dehautrie, in
the 86th year of her age, native of France and for last 30 yrs res of
Frederick/Died in this place Sun night 5th inst, after a short illness, Mrs.
Mary Doyle, old inhabitant, in the 80th year of her age/Died same day Abraham Sherwood, for some yrs res of this town, aged 43 yrs, native of Romney,
in the county of Kent, England/Died Wed last, Mrs. Elizabeth Lowe, aged inhabitant

350. FHB Apr 18 1829/Married in Balt, Sun evening last, by Rev Henshaw,
Philip Reich, to Miss Rebecca D. H. Ayres, both of Frederick/Married Tues
evening last in this city, by Rev Jonathan Helfenstein, Charles A. Gambrill,
of Balt Co, to Miss Ann M. Shriver, dau of hon. Abraham Shriver

351. FHB Apr 25 1829/Married Thurs 16 inst, by Rev David F. Schaeffer,
Michael Snouffer to Miss Caroline Miller, all of this co

352. FHB May 2 1829/Died 28th ult, George Rice, sen, after a few days
illness, in the 56th year of his age, leaving widow with a large family of
children

353. FHB May 9 1829/Married Sun last, by Rev David Martin, Peter Sowers to
Mrs. Pamilia Hartsock, all of this co/Married Tues morning by Rev D. F.
Schaeffer, Seth Nichols to Miss Catharine, ony dau of Henry Heichler, all of
this city/Chancery case - Michael Blessing, Lewis Motter and others, complainants, vs Frederick Dorsey and others, defendants - Object of the bill
is to obtain decree for sale of real estate of Michael Dorsey, Frederick Co,
decd, for payment of his debts. Michael Dorsey died intestate, leaving
following persons his heirs, to wit: Frederick Dorsey, Mary Ann Dorsey who
married James Love, Elizabeth who married Joseph Smith, John Dorsey, Henry
Dorsey, Michael Dorsey, Owen Dorsey and Harriet Dorsey. James Love could
not be found at his usual place of abode

354. FHB May 23 1829/Died 17th inst, after a protracted illness, Simon
Cronise, in the 43d year of his age, leaving 2 daus

355. FHB May 30 1829/Married Tues evening last at Carlisle, by Rev George
Duffield, Rev John W. McCullough of this city, to Miss Mary Louis Duncan, of
the former place/Died 18th inst at Annapolis, after a protracted and painful
illness, George Shaw, Esq. in the 39th year of his age - Md. Rep./Died at
Hagerstown 21st inst, after a few weeks illness, William Fitzhugh, Jr., Esq.
in the 42d year of his age, late Jackson Elector for this district/Died

Thurs morning last in the 81st year of his age, John Bruner of this city
/Died same day, Henry Hull, bricklayer, after a short illness

356. FHB Jun 6 1829/Married Thurs 28th ult by rev David F. Schaeffer, Peter
Degrange to Miss Louisa Catharine Ebbert, of this city/Died morning 27th
ult, Rev John G. Grobp, sen, pastor of the Evangelical Luth Church, Taney-
town, in the 70th year of his age, native of Germany, which he left in 1780,
and 3 yrs after came to this country. His public ministry lasted upwards of
30 yrs

357. FHB Jun 13 1829/Died Mon afternoon last, at the res of his mother, in
Gettysburg, James G. M'Neely, Esq formerly Attorney at Law of this town and
late Principal of the Frederick Academy, in the 34th year of his age, leaving widowed mother and sorrowing sisters. The mother had just lost to the
grave her son, Dr. Grier of Reading - Adams Sen.

358. FHB Jul 4 1829/Married Tues 23d ult by Rev Snethen, Charles C. Wor-
thington to Miss Ann Brashear, dau of Dr. Belt Brashear, both of this co
/Married Tues 23d ult by Rev D.F. Schaeffer, John Richter to Miss Catharine
Cookerly, both of this co/Married Sat evening last by Rev David Martin,
Jacob Dadisman to Miss Lydia Ann Storm, both of this city

359. FHB Jul 25 1829/Married at Uniontown Thurs 16th inst, by Rev Zollick-
offer, Dr. James Fisher, of Westiminster, to Miss Elizabeth M. Boyer, dau of
Dr. Thomas Boyer of the former place/Died Fri 17th inst, Charles Ridgely of
Hampton, late Governor of Md, in the 70th year of his age

360. FHB Aug 1 1829/Married Thurs evening last, by Rev James L. Higgins,
Francis Thomas Mealey to Miss Arie Shivers, all of this co/Died at Marseil-
les, France, very suddenly, 29 May last, Rev Michael de Bourgo Egan, Presi-
dent of Mount St. Mary's Seminary, near Emmitsburg, in this co. He sailed
from this country in Oct last for the benefit of his health

361. FHB Aug 8 1829/Married Tues morning last by Rev Jonathan Helfenstein,
Henry N. Tice to Miss Barbara Ann, dau of John Kunkell, Esq., all of this
city

362. FHB Aug 15 1829/Died at Belinda Springs, Wash Co, Tues Aug 11, in 18th
year of his age, Alexander Hamilton Richardson, eldest son of Davis Richardson, Esq. of this co, after a protracted illness of 10 months, a disease of
the pulmonary kind

363. FHB Aug 22 1829/Died Mon morning last, George Lease, of this city, in
the 57th year of his age

364. FHB Aug 29 1829/Married Sun 16th inst, by Rev J. A. Gere, George B.
Shope to Miss Louisa Kellar, all of this city/Died Wed morning 26th inst, in
the 77th year of her age, Mrs. Ann Mary Baltzell, consort of Jacob Baltzell,
of this town, native of this place, lived in wedlock upwards of 55 yrs,
leaving husband, 9 sons and 1 surviving dau/Died Tues morning, after a protracted illness, Dr. Henry Staley, of this city

365. FHB Sep 5 1829/Mrs. Roach, consort of Robert Roach, Esq., of this city, died Fri 28th ult, after an illness of a few weeks aged about 35 yrs, leaving husband and 6 small children, member Episc Meth - Examiner/Died Sat morning last at the res of her mother in New-Market, Miss Malinda Scott

366. FHB Sep 12 1829/Died Sun last in the 27th year of her age, Mrs. Elizabeth Zimmerman, consort of George Zimmerman, paper-maker, after an illness of about 2 weeks - Citizen/Col. Stephen Steiner died Tues evening last, after an illness of a few days, in the 61st year of his age, head of a regiment from this co during the late war, marched to Baltimore and endured the hardships of the camp - Citizen

367. FHB Sep 19 1829/Married Tues morning last by rev Wachter, John Walker, of Ohio, to Miss Elizabeth Kemp, 2nd dau of Capt. David Kemp, of this co /Died Sun last, aged 27 yrs, Mrs. Elizabeth Fout, consort of Lewis Fout, of this vicinity, just a few short months since she became a wife/Died recently at his res in this co, James Rice, Esq. an old citizen, for many yrs a magistrate of this co -·Citizen

368. FHB Sep 26 1829/Died Wed morning in 46th year of his age, Rev Jonathan Helfenstein, for many yrs Pastor of the German Reformed Church of this place. For 18 yrs he resided among us; his labours embraced four congregations, to whom he preached in German and English. He left a widow and 11 children/Died Fri 18th inst, after a long and painful illness of the pulmonary kind, Mrs. Susan Geasee, widow of Jacob Geasee, of Liberty, who died 16 Aug/Died Thurs 17 inst, after a few days illness, at his res on Israels Creek, Nicholas Hoy, Jr., aged about 30 yrs/Died Sat evening in this city, Francis Hartz, after a few days illness, aged about 84 yrs

369. FHB Oct 3 1829/George W. Falconer, New Market, offers reward for apprentice to blacksmith's trade, named Benjamin Williams, now about 20 yrs of age, 5 ft 9-10 inch

370. FHB Oct 10 1829/Died Fri 24th Sep, Fayette Johnson, formerly res of Balt Co, in the 47th year of his age, leaving wife and children. Unless well acquainted he was remarkably reserved and diffident, though when friendships were formed his attachments were warm and sincere

371. FHB Oct 24 1829/Married Wed 14th inst by Rev Stone, Wm. V. Morgan to Miss Sarah Broadrup, all of this city/Married Mon evening last, by Rev J. W. M'Cullough, Henry Sturgis to Miss Ann Eliza Sinn, all of this city/Died 18th inst, after a lingering illness at the res of Wm. Schley, Esq., in this city, Gen. Samuel Ringgold of Wash Co, Md, in the 60th year of his age, elected to state and national office/Died near Petersville in this co, 13th inst, Lingan Boteler, aged 56/Died at his res in Prince George's Co, Md, in the 75th year of his age, Col. Wm. Dent Beall, distinguished officer of the Revolutionary army; served in the state legislature

372. FHB Oct 31 1829/Died Sun morning last, Peter Degrange, sen., of this town, at an advanced age/Died same day in the vicinity of this place, Philip Feaga, at an advanced age

45

373. FHB Nov 7 1829/Married Tues evening last, by Rev John A. Stone, Henry
B. Eaty of Jefferson Co, Va, to Miss Lucy Ann Cromwell, dau of Joseph M.
Cromwell, of this co/Married Thurs evening 29th ult, by Rev Hitt, Wesley
Jones to Miss Margaret Poole, both of this co/Died Mon morning last, Peter
Fout, of this place, at an advanced age

374. FHB Nov 14 1829/Married Tues inst by rev W. Armstrong, Mr. B. A. Cunningham, to Miss Rebecca Hasselback, both of Frederick Co/Died Wed morning
inst, Mrs. Susan Mantz, consort of John Mantz, of this city/Died in Louisville, Jefferson Co, Georgia, Sat 17th ult, John Jacob Schley, in the 77th
year of his age, born in Frederick Town, where he continued to reside until
the winter of 1793, when he removed to Louisville, Georgia. He left an aged
widow and 8 children, and many grand children/Died Fri morning 6th inst,
Upton L. Dorsey, aged about 30 yrs, leaving widow and children. He com-
plained the night previous and on the following morning expired suddenly,
without a struggle/Died in Lisbon, Anne Arundel Co, Thurs 5th inst, Charles
Banks, in the 20th year of his age

375. FHB Nov 21 1829/John Hanshew residing in Frederick-Town, offers reward
for apprentice to house carpenter's trade named Joseph Measel, about 19 yrs
of age, 5 ft 6-7 inch

376. FHB Nov 28 1829/Married Tues last by Rev Grog, Cornelius Staley, of
this co, to Miss Rosanna Schnebly of Wash Co/Died Sun night last in the 35th
year of his age, John A. Donne, resident of this city the greatest part of 5
yrs, Principal of Frederick Female Academy, greatly suffering in the last
stages of his disease - Examiner

377. FHB Dec 5 1829/Col. John M'Pherson died in this city, Wed last, in the
69th year of his age, after an illness of a few days. He was a native of
Pennsylvania, came to Frederick in 1781. Not long before the conclusion of
the rev war he received a lieutenant's commission in the service of his native state. He came to Frederick, as an agent for the supply of prisoners,
then quartered here. He married in 1783 which confirmed his residence in
Frederick, where he has since lived, served as associate judge of Frederick
co - Citizen/Married Thurs of last week, by Rev D. F. Schaeffer, Geo. Smith,
Jr., to Miss Lydia Baucher, all of this co/Married same evening by Rev John
A. Gere, George K. Fox to Miss Mary Ann E. Mills, all of this co

378. FHB Dec 12 1829/Married Tues evening 1st inst by Rev Engler, Isaac
Slingluff to Miss Juba Ann Engler, dau of Philip Engler, all of this co

379. FHB Dec 19 1829/Married Thurs last by Rev Linthicum, Cornelius Mercer,
of Balt Co, to Miss Sarah Ann Gaither, only dau of Major Samuel Gaither, of
Anne Arundel co/Died morning of 8th inst, in the 55th year of his age, John
R. Magruder, of this co, leaving wife and children/Died morning of 10th
inst, Mrs. Elizabeth Perry, in the 34th year of her age, wife of William
Perry, of this co. For many years Mr. Perry has been deprived of his sight
(and apparently depended greatly on his wife).

380. FHB Jan 2 1830/Married Thurs last by Rev D.F. Schaeffer, John Engel to
Miss Christina Schaeffer/Married same day by same, George Eader, to Miss

Mary Ann Hopwood, all of this co/Married evening of same day by same, John
Cooke of Lancaster, Pa, to Miss Christianna E. Mantz, of this city/Married
same evening by same, Benjamin Ebert of Lancaster, Pa, to Miss Caroline M.
Birely, of this city/Married same evening by Rev Michael Wachter, John
Zimmerman, to Miss Miranda Myers, all of this co/Died Wed evening last, Mrs.
Susan Kemp, consort of Col. Henry Kemp, in the 57th year of her age, wife
and mother

381. FHB Jan 9 1830/Married Thurs morning last by Rev John A. Gere, Robert
Roach to Miss Mary Eliza Bausman, all of this city/Died Thurs morning, after
a lingering illness, Mrs. Ann Margaret Leatherman, relict of Henry Leatherman, in the 76th year of her age, and 50th year of her residence in this
city, member of German Reformed Church from her earliest yrs, as had been
her parents who with many others of the same religion, near a century since,
migrated from the Palatinate on the Rhine, and contributed largely to the
erection of the church/Chancery case - Benjamin Biggs, John Pittinger and
others vs John Biggs, Joseph Biggs and others - Object of bill is to obtain
decree for sale of part of real estate of John Biggs, decd, for payment of
debts. The bill states that defendants Jacob Eagler is adm'r and heirs of
the decd are parties defendants, to wit: Jacob Plaine and wife Mary, Benjamin Peck and wife Caroline, John Biggs, Joseph Biggs, and Miles Plaine, on
the ground that they reside in Ohio

382. FHB Jan 16 1830/Married Tues evening last, by Rev Devos, James Peter,
Esq. to Miss Susanna, dau of late John O'Neal, Esq., all of Mont Co

383. FHB Jan 23 1830/Monday last Daniel Fout, a young man of this vicinity,
in returning home from town, was thrown from his horse and so much injured
that he expired in a few minutes/Married Tues evening last by Rev Schaeffer,
David B. Devitt to Miss Elizabeth Fout, all of this city

384. FHB Jan 30 1830/Married 17 inst by Rev John H. Smaltz, David Gilbert to
Miss Margaret Koontz/Married 24th inst by same, Charles W. Todd to Miss
Marcellea Bonham/Married Thurs morning last by same, Hugh Cunningham to Miss
Rebecca Gettinger, all of Frederick Co/Married same day by same, Henry Yokey
to Miss Mary Jacobs, both of Carroll's Manor, Frederick Co/Died Sat night
last, after a short illness, Richard M. Hardesty, in the 21st year of his
age. About 16 months ago this gentleman left the residence of his friends
in Prince George's Co and came to Frederick to prosecute the study of the
law, in which he was an assiduous student until his last illness/Died evening of Wed 20th inst, Doct. William Adams, age unknown, but from circumstances, supposed to be upwards of 100 yrs. He was a native of Ireland,
where he resided til qualified for the practice of medicine. At age 20 he
removed to America, during the French war of 1744-63, and was for some time
surgeon in the service of Sir William Johnston, the British colonial agent
for Indian affairs, in the, now, state of New York. For more than 70 yrs he
was a practising physician, for a greater part of that time a resident in
the city of Schnectady. Relinquishing his duties of his profession he removed to Rochester, N.Y. In August last he came to Frederick Town, on a
visit to one of his grand daughters; but, when at Ellicott's Mils, received
a fall, under the painful effects of which he lingered till his death - Ex-
aminer/Died in Balt on 23d inst, Miss Sarah Lee Potts, dau of late Wm.

Potts, Esq. of Frederick Co; interred in Episc grave yard of Frederick, near the spot which contains those of a numerous family, of which she was the last

385. FHB Feb 6 1830/Married Mon last by Rev John A. Gere, Rev Francis A. M'Neill to Miss Mary Cronise, dau of Simon Cronise, decd, all of this co/Died Mon last in the 54th year of his age, Henry Sinn, of this town/Died morning of 27th ult, at her res in New-Market, Mrs. Elizabeth Pitts, relict of late Rev John Pitts, in the 50th year of her age

386. FHB Feb 13 1830/Married Tues last by Rev Michael Wachter, Samuel Fleming of John to Miss Hannah Koons, all of this place/Chancery case - Daniel Flook vs John Flook, Philip Bentz and Lydia Bentz his wife, and others. Object of the bill is to obtain decree for sale of real esate of late John Flook the elder, decd, who alledgedly died intestate. The bill professes to name heirs of intestate and that the defendant John Flook, one of the sons of said intestate was advanced by said intestate in his life time $861.01, as were several children advanced; also that defendant John the son resides in Ohio, and Philip Bentz and Lydia Bentz his wife (which said Lydia is stated to be the ony child of intestate's dau Mary who married Frederick Doub, but who died in the lifetime of said intestate, leaving the said Lydia her only child, reside in Kentucky

387. FHB Feb 20 1830/Married Thurs last by rev D. F. Schaeffer, Jacob Ramsburg, to Miss Elizabeth Ramsburg, both of this co/Married Thurs morning 18th inst at Buckeys Town by Rev John H. Smaltz, Joseph Koons to Miss Rebecca Shuh, both of this co/Died Thurs 11 inst Henry Bantz, sen., Esq at an advanced age, of this town/Died Fri last Miss Eliza Lyon, dau of Dr. Isaac Lyon, of this place, after a short illness/Died Sun last, Mrs. Galt, consort of William Galt, near Woodsborough/Died Thurs 11th inst, Mrs. Catharine Lott, in the 79th year of her age/Died Mon last in the 70th year of her age, Mrs. Esther Gomber, consort of John Gomber/Died yesterday morning of a pulmonary affection, Thomas H. Fleming, of this co/Conrad Dudderer, Frederick Co, offers reward for apprentice to farming business named Joseph Close, now about 17 yrs of age

388. FHB Mar 6 1830/Married 28 Feb 1830 by Rev John A. Gere, John T. Waters to Miss Mary Ann Moss, all of this co/Married 2 Mar by same, Richard Mackubin of Balt to Miss Juliana R.M., 2nd dau of Rezin Rawles, of Frederick Co

389. FHB Mar 13 1830/Died in Balt Tues last, Baker Johnson Ross, 2nd son of William Ross, Esq. of this city, in the 21st year of his age. A few months ago he left his native town in the fulness of strength. He completed a course of collegiate instruction at Dickinson College, in the fall of 1823 /Died Fri 5th inst, in the 78th year of her age, Mrs. Catharine Schley, relict of late Thomas Schley

390. FHB Mar 20 1830/Married near Randall Town, Balt Co, Tues 9th inst, by Rev Choate, George Mering, Jr, Esq. of Big Pipe Creek, in this co, to Miss Rebecca Chapman, of the former place/Married Thurs 4th inst by Rev David Engler, Cornelius Conway, Esq. to Miss Nancy Pfoutz, dau of Samuel Pfoutz,

all of this co/Married Sun evening last by Rev John H. Smaltz, John L. Levy
to Miss Sarah R. Saunders, all of this city

391. FHB Mar 27 1830/Married Tues evening last, by Rev Reese, Daniel M.
Kemp, to Miss Susan M. Stauffer, dau of Joseph Stauffer, all of Frederick
Co/Married Tues evening last, by Rev John H. Smaltz, John Brunner of Jacob,
merchant, to Miss Sophia Doll, all of this city/Married Thurs evening last,
by same, John Whip, from the Manor, to Miss Magdalena Breedy, of this city

392. FHB Apr 10 1830/Married Tues evening last, by Rev Daniel Zollicoffer,
Joseph Poole to Miss Esther Slingluff, dau of Jesse Slinghuff, Esq. all of
this co

393. FHB Apr 17 1830/Married Thurs 8th inst by Rev Joshua Jones, John Derr,
Jr. to Miss Eliza Lugenbeel, both of this co/Married Thurs evening last, by
Rev David Martin, William J. Thomson to Miss Margaretta Davis, both of this
city

394. FHB Apr 24 1830/Married at Graceham 13th inst. by Rev John A. Gere, Dr.
Leander W. Goldsborough to Miss Sarah Ann Duncan, dau of late Capt. Duncan,
late of Balt/Married 8th inst by Rev John H. Smaltz, William Price to Miss
Ann G. Kohlenberg, all of this co/Married 22d inst by same, William Rice to
Miss Rebecca Bierley, both of this city/Mrs. Harriet Kemp, wife of Daniel
Kemp of H., after a short illness of a few days, died Wed 21st inst

395. FHB May 1 1830/Married Thurs evening 15th ult, by Rev Riley, Washington Nicodemus, Esq., youngest son of Capt. Philip Nicodemus, to Miss Elizabeth A., eldest dau of Andrew Nicodemus, all of this co/Married Thurs evening last by Rev John A. Gere, Samuel J. Lindsay, of Harpers Ferry, Va, to
Miss Eleanor Ann Rohr of this city

396. FHB May 8 1830/Married evening of 27th ult by Rev Bosler, Dr. Andrew
Annan to Miss Eliza Motter, dau of Lewis Motter, Esq., all of Emmitsburg
/Married same evening by Rev Hickley, John Jarboe to Miss Jane Patterson,
all of this co/Married Sun 25th ult by Rev Brute, Philip J. Cahill, printer,
to Miss Sophia A.C. Elder, all of this co/Married Tues last by same, Jacob
Costigar to Miss Cecelia Elder

397. FHB May 15 1830/Married Tues last by Rev David Martin, Thomas Howard of
this co, to Miss Eleanor Fleming, of this city/Died Tues last, Nicholas
Lease, of this co/Died same day, Miss Elizabeth Steiner, dau of Henry Steiner, of this city/Died Tues week last, near Petersville, Francis A. Hamilton,
in the 28th year of his age

398. FHB May 22 1830/Married 8th inst by Rev D.F. Schaeffer, Emanuel Thomas,
Esq. of New-Town, to Miss Ann Catharine, dau of George Remsburg, esq. of
this co/Married Tues last, at Martinsburg, Va, Doct. Milton Johnson, of this
co, to Miss Jane Kennedy, of the former place/Died Tues last, in this town,
John Hart, saddler, in the 36th year of his age

399. FHB May 29 1830/Died 2d inst in the 51st year of her age, Mrs. Rachel
Gist, widow of late Independent Gist of this co, for a number of yrs

afflicted with cancer. For last 10 months her dissolution had been almost daily looked for/Married Thurs evening last by Rev Albert Helfenstein of Balt, Zachariah T. Simmons, merchant, to Miss Louisa C. Helfenstein, dau of late Rev Jonathan Helfenstein of this city/Married same evening, Samuel P. Davidson, editor of the Taney-Town Regulator to Miss Lydia Rate of this co/Married same day by Rev John A. Gere, Joshua Souder to Miss Margaret Kessler, all of this co

400. FHB Jun 19 1830/Married Tues 8th inst by Rev J. R. Keach, Charles Hammond Raitt, of Balt, to Miss Cassandra Whitaker, only dau of Samuel Whitaker, Esq. of Harford Co/Married Tues evening last by Rev D. F. Schaeffer, Peter Hoff, to Miss Elizabeth Kandall, all of this city/Died Fri 11th inst, in the 51st year of her age, Mrs. Mary Magdalene Greenwald, consort of Christian Greenwald, of this vicinity, afflicted for nearly ten yrs past with that lingering and burdensome disease, the dropsy; and had the operation commonly called tapping, performed upon her no less that 56 different times!

401. FHB Jun 26 1830/Died at his res on Linganore Thurs 17th inst, Nathan Hammond of Philip, in the 60th year of his age, leaving wife and several children/Died in city of Balt, on 16th inst, of pulmonary affection, Frederick A. Gabhart, of this city, in the 32d year of his age; remains brought to Frederick, and interred in cemetery of the German Reformed Church

402. FHB Jul 17 1830/Married 10th inst by Rev D.F. Schaeffer, Jacob Ridgely to Mrs. Cresa Ann Wagner, all of this co/Died in Balt on 8th inst at res of her son-in-law, R. B. Taney, Esq. Mrs. Phebe A. Key, at an advanced period of life. She, we believe, was a native of Frederick Town

403. FHB Jul 24 1830/Married Tues last by Rev J. A. Gere, Michael Shank to Miss Jane A. Maddox, both of Va/Married same day, by same, John Scholl to Miss Sarah Ann Coxen, all of this co/Married Sun last by Rev D.F. Schaeffer, Mr. A. Padgett to Miss Elizabeth Eader

404. FHB Jul 31 1830/Married 23d inst by Rev. D. F. Schaeffer, Henry Young to Miss Susan G. Hilton/Married Sunday evening last, by same, Jacob Keefer to Miss Rebecca Biggs, all of this place/Married Tues morning, by Rev Smaltz, Nimrod Bantz to Miss Mary Harding, all of this place/Married Thurs last by rev Baugher, Henry McDuell, to Miss Magdalena Smith, both of this co/Died Sun last at the res of her father, Mrs. Rebecca S. Brien, wife of John M'Pherson Brien, of Wash Co, and dau of J. Meredith, Esq. of Balt

405. FHB Aug 7 1830/Married Thurs evening last, by Rev Jackson, Nicholas A. Randall to Miss Mary E. Worthington, dau of William Worthington, of this city

406. FHB Aug 14 1830/Chancery case - John M'Aleer vs Mathew Warttman & others - object is to obtain decree for sale of real estate of John M. Warttman, decd, who died intestate. The bill states that Matthew Warttman, a brother of the intestate and one of the defendants, resides in Ohio

407. FHB Aug 28 1830/Died in Liberty-Town Mon 23rd inst, Mrs. Ann M. Willson, wife of Richard A. Willson, in the 42nd year of her age, leaving husband and children

408. FHB Sep 4 1830/Married Tues morning last by Rev David F. Schaeffer, A.M., Lewis Fout to Miss Mary Ann Late, dau of late Jacob Late, Esqr, both of this co

409. FHB Sep 11 1830/Married at Middletown, Frederick Co, 31st Aug by Rev J.C. Bucher, Jacob Kuhn, to Miss Lydia Ann Beckenbaugh, all of Frederick Co/Married 2nd inst by same, Jacob Ahult to Mary Ann Smith, all of Frederick Co

410. FHB Sep 18 1830/Married Sun last by Rev James G. Hammer, Thomas Brashear, to Miss Louisa Rohr, dau of Jacob Rohr, Esq., all of this city /Married same day by Rev John H. Smaltz, Isaac Crum, to Miss Catharine Kessler, both of this co

411. FHB Sep 25 1830/Married Sat last by Rev John H. Smaltz, Jonathan Forrest Covell to Miss Catharine Jacobs, both of this co/Married Mon last by Rev M'Elroy, James U. Armour to Miss Charlotte, dau of late Jos. Fleming, all of this city

412. FHB Oct 2 1830/Married Tues last by Rev Frederick Stier, Joseph Reatleary to Miss Martha Creager, both of this co/Died Thurs evening 23rd ult, after a short and severe illness of 3 days, in the 16th year of his age, Richard C. Cromwell, youngest son of Joseph M. Cromwell, Esq/Died Fri 24th ult, George Adam Straeffer, of this co, in the 33rd year of his age, victim to Typhus Fever, with which he was attacked about a week before his death. At an early age he attached himself to the Luth Church. Many numerous friends and relatives, some of whom live in the Western States/Died suddenly on Wed morning last, Mrs. Mary Smith, aged lady of this town/Died same day after a protracted and painful illness, Woodward Evitt, of this vicinity, an an advanced age – Citizen/From Hagerstown Herald - Died on the morning of 22 Sep at Morristown, Ohio, after a few days of severe indisposition, William C. Thomson, of this place, in the 29th year of his age who resided but a few year among us

413. FHB Oct 16 1830/Married Sun evening 3d inst by Rev D.F. Shaeffer, William Engelbrecht, to Miss Susan Winter, both of this city/Married Tues evening 12th inst, by Rev Stilenger, at Mount Saint Mary's Seminary, John B. Keepers, to Miss Elizabeth Cratin

414. FHB Oct 23 1830/Married Thurs 14th inst in Balt by Rev C.C. Peise, Dr. Edward Miller, of Frederick, to Miss Harriet C. Watson, of Balt/Married Tues 12th inst, by Rev David F. Schaeffer, Otho Fout, to Miss Catharine Carum, both of this co/Married 19th inst by Rev Smaltz, Augustus F. Ebert, to Miss Elizabeth M. Bantz, dau of Gideon Bantz, esq. all of this place

415. FHB Oct 30 1830/Married Sun 24th inst in Frederick by Rev Peters, George Nichols, jr. to Miss Mary Ann Beavans, both of this co

51

416. FHB Nov 13 1830/Died 9th inst after a tedious sickness of several months, Mrs. Susan Reidenmayer, consort of Conrad Reidenmayer, old inhabitant of this city

417. FHB Nov 20 1830/Married 2d inst by Rev Wacher, George Devilbiss to Miss Mary Creager, both of this co/Died 22d Oct at Corn Hill Farm, near Merom, Indiana, at the res of her father, Margaret Anabella Snethen, 3d dau of Rev Nicholas Snethen, formerly of Frederick Co, Md, aged 13 yrs and 16 days, after a severe attack of inflammatory bilious fever/Died Mon morning, 8th inst, at Fredericksburg, Va, in the 35th year of her age, Mrs. Sarah Ann Miller, consort of Benjamin M. Miller, leaving husband and 2 children, resident among us for a few years - Pol. Arena/Died Tues morning 9th inst, Mrs. Catherine Lembrecht, of this city, im the 28th year of her age

418. FHB Nov 27 1830/Married Tues evening last, by rev David Martin, Dr. Albert Ritchie, to Miss Catherine L. Davis, all of this city/Married same evening, by Rev Armstrong, George Bowlus, esq. of this co, to Miss Ann, dau of late Thomas Benson, esq. of Mont co

419. FHB Dec 4 1830/Married Tues 16th ult, Dr. G.W. West, of Petersville, to Miss Eliza Pratt of Newtown, both of Frederick Co, Md/Married Thurs evening last at Middletown by Rev Reck, Jacob Hart of this city to Miss Mary, dau of Caspar Herring of the former place

420. FHB Dec 18 1830/Married in New York Thurs 9th inst, by Rev Dr. Spring, Rev James G. Hammer, Pastor of the Presby Church, in this city, to Miss Jane, dau of late capt. Thomas M'Elderry of Balt/Married Tues evening 7th inst by Rev James L. Higgins, George Kline to Miss Sarah Elizabeth, 2d dau of late Frederick Poole, all of this co/Died 3d inst, Daniel Sheffey, esq., formerly member of congress from Virginia (once worked at the trade of shoemaking in this city)/Died at Taney Town, Md., on 5th inst, Daniel Boyle. esq, in the 66th year of his age, who long filled the office of P. Master /Died Sun last, Mary Ann, dau of Jacob Geaty, of this city, in the 12th year of her age/Equity case - Elizabeth Howard and Philemon M. Smith vs Mary Hall, James Mullikan and Ann his wife, James Torrance and Ann his wife, and others. Object of proceedings is to obtain decree for sale of certain premises mortgged by late Baruch Hall, decd, to the complainants. The bill states that the death of said mortgager, and the devise of his estate, after certain devises and bequests, to his relations, and enumerates them, of whom the said Ann Mullikan wife of James Mullikan, and said Ann Torrance wife of said James Torrance are two, both residing in Kentucky or somewhere in the U.S. outside Md

421. FHB Dec 25 1830/Married Thurs last by Rev Michael Wachter, Samuel Krise to Miss Mary Ann Slummer(?), all of this co/Married Tues evening 14th inst by rev Gere, George W. Hoffman, to Miss Catharine Buckey, dau of Peter Buckey, all of this co

THE REPUBLICAN GAZETTE

The Republican Gazette and General Advertiser, Frederick-town, published by
Mathias Bartgis

422. RGM Jan 1 1820/John Walter, near Emmittsburgh, offers reward for
apprentice bound to shoe making business, Jacob Martin, about 18, 5 ft, 2
inch

423. RGM Jan 22 1820/Chancery case - John Ritchie, William Ritchie, Robert
McClery and others vs. John Ritchie, Abner Ritchie, Eleanor Ritchie, Matilda
Ritchie, Joshua Ritchie, John William Ott, Mary C. Ott, Mary Knight, William
McCleery, Michael McClanaghan & Susan his wife. Object of bill is to obtain
decree to sell improved lot in Frederick Town and for distribution of money
arising therefrom. Mary Ritchie of Frederick Co, widow, died 1818 intestate, leaving complainants and defendants her legal representatives

424. RGM Mar 18 1820/Jacob Reed about 1 mile from Frederick Town, offers
reward for black boy bound to farming business, Samuel Flint, 19, 5 ft 6-7
inches, slender

425. RGM Nov 11 1820/Died Tues morning last in 62d year of his age, John
Fessler, Senr.; interred in Luth burial ground. He was a res of this place
upwards of 40 yrs, many yrs a vestryman, for 18 yrs an elder to Luth
Congregation

426. RGM Jan 6 1821 Equity Case: - Jonah Buffington and Magdalena his wife,
John Coblentz & Elizabeth his wife, Solomon Renner & Barbara his wife,
Thompson M'Crey & Mary his wife, and Henry Ecard vs. Jacob Coblentz, Jacob
Coblentz, Jun., Peter Coblentz & Catherine Coblentz. Object is to obtain
decree of sale of real estate of Michael Ecard, who died intestate, seized
and possessed in fee simple of real estate that he left Magdalena wife of
Jonah Buffington, Elizabeth wife of John Coblentz, Barbara wife of Solomon
Renner, Mary wife of Thompson McCrey, Catherine wife of Jacob Coblentz, and
Henry Ecard, his children and heirs at law. Catherine Coblentz, wife of
Jacob Coblentz died since the death of her said father, leaving Jacob Coblentz, Jr., Peter Coblentz, and Catherine Coblentz, her children and heirs,
all under age of 21, and who reside out of state of Md. Jacob Coblentz is
living out of state of Md.

427. RGM Jan 20 1821/Died Wed 10th inst, Miss Elizabeth Christian Potts,
dau of late William Potts, Esq. of Fred. Co/Died suddenly Sat evening last,
Mrs. Elizabeth Cromwell, wife of Richard Cromwell, of this co; interred in
burying ground of German Reformed Church

428. RGM Jan 27 1821/Died Mon last, Adam Ollix, aged 93 yrs, res of this
city , upwards of 60 yrs/Died same at his res in this co, Henry Jenkins,
aged 37 yrs, of pulmonary complaint, leaving widow and 3 infant children;
interred in Roman Cath burying ground; sermon delivered by Rev Malave

429. RGM Feb 10 1821/Married Thurs evening 1st inst by Rev Alfred Griffith,
Evan Hopkins to Miss Ann Patterson, all of this place/Chancery case - David
Baltzell, Lawrence Baltzell, by his next friend Jacob Geesey, John Burkhart
and Rebecca Burkhart, his wife and Elias Spoon vs. George Baltzell, Michael

53

Rice & Elizabeth Rice his wife, Susanna Baltzell, John Baltzel, John Geesey and Catharine Geesey, his wife, John M'Hugh & Margaret M'Hugh his wife, Jacob Shryock & Ann Shryock his wife, Elizabeth Baltzell, Samuel Baltzell, John Main, Jacob Layman & Bean S. Pigman. Object of bill is to obtain decree for sale of tract called The Resurvey on Baltzell's Content. Jacob Baltzeel decd, by his last will devised a legacy to David Baltzell, Lawrence Baltzell, Rebecca Baltzell, now Rebecca Burkhart, and to Mary Bartzell, who afterwards married Elias Spoon and hath since died. Since the death of said Jacob Baltzell, several of his children have died, to wit: (1) Jacob Baltzell, leaving children, Margaret Baltzell who since m John M'Hugh, Ann Baltzell who since m Jacob Shryock, Elizabeth Baltzel and Samuel Baltzell; (2) Mary Baltzell who m Elias Spoon, without leaving any children; (3) Peter Baltzell without leaving any children. George Baltzell resides in Kentucky, Michael Rice and Elizabeth Rice reside in Ohio, Susanna Baltzell resides in Ohio, John Baltzell resides in Kentucky

430. RGM Feb 17 1821/Married Sun evening last by Rev D. F. Schaeffer, Jacob Metzgar, to Mrs.Elizabeth Gardner, widow of the late Henry Gardner, all of this city/Married at Rose Hill, Jefferson co, Va, by Rev E. R. S. Pippon, Sopus Mockaboy to Miss Jemima Tucker all of that place

431. RGM Apr 7 1821/From Lexington, Ky, March 1 1821. Died on 16 ult after a long and tedious illness, Henry Johnson, stranger who came to the house of James M'Connell of this place, about the middle of October and requested lodging for a few weeks, to enable him to enjoy retirement, and derive also the advantages of a milk diet. He intimated to Mrs. M'Connell, his unwillingness to communicate to his friends his situation, until he should be recruited sufficient to prosecute his journey to New Orleans; adding at the same time, his mother and other relatives lived in the state of Md. Mr. Johnson left in the hands of Mr. M'Connell, about 1600 dollars, a gold watch, cloths and a I believe a horse

432. RGM Apr 21 1821/Died 1st inst after an illness of about 6 weeks, Henry Jarboe, esq. of this co, leaving a widow and 2 children/Died Thurs last, Jacob Medart, old inhabitant of this town/Died on morning of 5th inst, after a lingering and severe illness, at his res in Unity township, William Findley, hero of the rev. and rep. in congress from this district

433. RGM Apr 28 1821/Married Mon evening last, by Rev Maleve, Jacob Brugey to Miss Catharine Hardts, all of this town

434. RGM May 5 1821/Married Mon evening last by Rev Johns, Frederick Markey to Miss Elizabeth Dill, all of this town

435. RGM Jun 30 1821/Married Thurs last by Rev Davison, Woodward Evitt, Esq. to Mrs. Margaret Tise, all of this city

436. RGM Jul 7 1821/Married Tues evening last by Rev Jonathan Helfenstein, James Weaver, to Miss Henrietta Trisler, dau of George Trisler, Esq. all of this town/Married Tues evening last by Rev Jonathan Helfenstein, William Hayser of Chambersburg, to Miss Elizabeth Bentz, dau of George Bentz, of this place/Married Thurs evening 21st ult by Rev David F. Schaeffer, James

THE REPUBLICAN GAZETTE

Rice, to Miss Rebecca Drill, all of Frederick co/Died Tues morning last,
Richard White, citizen of this town

437. RGM Jul 14 1821/Married evening of 7th inst by Rev Davidson, Dr.
Thomas Springer, to Miss Mary Keller, all of Fred. co/Died Fri 6th inst Mrs.
Sarah McPherson wife of Col. John McPherson of this town, in the 55th year
of her age

438. RGM Jul 21 1821/Died Sun night last, Geo. W. Powers, a young man of
this town, after a few days illness; buried with masonic honors in English
Presby burial ground/Died Wed last, Adam Shisler, Jr. in the 54th year of
his age, of this town

439. RGM Jul 28 1821/Married Sun night last, by Rev P. Davidson, Samuel
McDade to Miss Elizabeth Asper, all of this city

440. RGM Aug 11 1821/Married Thurs evening last by Rev Richard Hunt, Lewis
Cross to Miss Charlotte Jones, all of this city/Died near Middle-town, Wed
8th inst, George Motter, Junr

441. RGM Aug 18 1821/Died Sun last, Mrs. Loranar Ragan, aged 77 yrs, buried
at English Episc Church/Died Thurs last near this place, Miss Margaret Smith

442. RGM Aug 31 1821/Married Sun 12th inst by Rev Maleve, Peter McKiernan
to Miss Mary Stonebraker, all of this co/Died Sun morning last, Mrs. Charlotte Birely, wife of Valentine Birely, and dau of Francis Mantz, of this
city/Died Wed last, in this town, Peter Braunsburg/Died same day, infant
child of John Boleston

443. RGM Sep 1 1821/Died near Frederick on 30th ult, Mrs. Robertson, wife
of James Robertson, leaving husband, son and dau/Died near Frederick, early
in morning of 31st ult, Mrs. Boone, wife of Alexius Boone/Died in Frederick
31st ult, at 9 o'clock, A.M., Mrs. Harriet Tyler, wife of Dr. Wm. Bradley
Tyler

444. RGM Sep 8 1821/Married Tues evening last, 4th inst by Rev J. Helfenstein, Charles Humrickhouse, of Hagers Town, to Miss Maria C. Levy of this
co

445. RGM Sep 15 1821/Married Thurs 9th inst by Rev Maleve, David Young, to
Miss Margaret Jones, all of this place/Married Sun evening, John Stoffel, to
Miss Nancy Skinner, all of this co/Died Wed 5th inst, Pierce Woods, esq.;
his death was occasioned by a fall/Died Sat 8th inst in 31st year of his
age, Perry W. Beall, son of Elisha Beall, and brother to the Sheriff of this
co/Died Tues 11th inst, Capt. William Campbell, wealthy and respectable
citizen of this co/Died on evening of Wed 12th inst, Michael Baltzell, Sen.,
at an advanced age/Died Wed 12th inst, Jacob Smith, aged 23 yrs

446. RGM Sep 22 1821/Died Thurs last, Mrs. Hoffman, widow of late Francis
Hoffman, decd/Died at Harpers ferry, Va, Mon 10th inst, Henry Kenney, native
of county Roscommon, Ireland, aged 26 yrs; remains deposited in Roman Cath
grave yard of this town, leaving wife and 2 small children/Died at Phila,

Thurs night, 30th ult, in 64th year of his age, after a lingering disease, Col. John F. Mercer, West River, Md./Died Sun evening last, at Shepherd-town, Va, in 20th year of his age, Samuel Bell, printer

447. RGM Sep 29 1821/Died Sat 16th inst at his res on Monocacy, Independent Gist, son of General Mordecai Gist, of Charleston, S. Carolina

448. RGM Oct 6 1821/Married Tues last by Rev D. F. Schaeffer, George ..ain, Junr to Mrs. Mary Klein, both of Fred. Co/Died Sun morning last, John Doll in the 45th year of his age, inhabitant of this city/Died same day, John Holl, aged 37/Died Wed last, near Frederick, Adam Snook, aged 71/Died same day, near Frederick, Peter Brunner, aged 97/Died Thurs last near Frederick, Miss Susanna Smith, aged 59

449. RGM Oct 13 1821/Died Tues last, Jacob Denner, aged 48, an European by birth/Died Wed last, Mrs. Mary Whip, consort of George Whip of this co, in the 39th year of her age/Died Sun last a dau of John Brunner, aged 2 yrs, 7 months

450. RGM Oct 20 1821/Died Wed morning at Annapolis, after a painful ill-ness, Hon. William Kelty, Chancellor of ths state of Md, in the 64th year of his age/Died Wed last, Adam Weaver. He emigrated to this country from Germany about 2 yrs ago; interred in Luth burying ground when Rev Shober delivered a pathetic address/Died Wed 3d inst, Dennis Magruder, son of Capt. Ely Brashear of this co, aged 12 yrs/Died Wed 10th inst, John Eckis of Taney-town, aged 82 yrs/Died Fri 17th inst, General John Ross Key, officer of the Rev. and inhabitant of this co/Died Sun night last, Catharine Stephens, aged 33 yrs, wife of Joseph Stephens of Carroll's Manor/Died Wed last, Mr. T. Jones, sen., long an inhabitant of this co

451. RGM Oct 27 1821/Died 21st Oct, George Smith, aged 88 yrs, 9 months, long an inhabitant of this co/Died same day Jacob Zuck in 32nd year of his age, leaving wife and 5 small children/Died recently near Westminster, Mrs. Elizabeth Reese, consort of Andrew Reese, of this co, in 62d year of her age/Died in Marblehead, Benjamin Dennis, aged 86. He lived to fight the battles of his country in 4 different wars; and in the late war, at 76 years of age, acted as gunner and officer on board several different privateers /Married Sun 14th inst, Mr. Keller, to Miss Mary Herring, both of this co/Married at Westminster in this co, on same day by Rev Greave(?), Henry Geaty to Miss Nancy Wilburn/Married Tues evening last by Rev Davidson, David B. Devitt, to Miss Ann Mantz, dau of Isaac Mantz, Esq., all of this city

452. RGM Nov 3 1821/Died 23d ult, Miss Hannah Baer of this place/Died Thurs last Mrs. Catharine Kalbfleish, aged 81

453. RGM Nov 10 1821/Married Sun last by Rev Schaeffer, Jacob Poffenberg, to Miss Mary Neff, all of this co

454. RGM Nov 17 1821/The body of Miss Eliza Myers was found in the head race of the mill belonging to Walter Poole, whose family she had lived a long time before her death. There is no certainty of the cause which led to her death; verdict of inquest: lost her life in a state of mental derange-

THE REPUBLICAN GAZETTE

ment/Died Sat morning in 10th inst in New Market, Francis Deakins Wayman, in
24th year of his age, res of Merryland Tract, near New Town (Trap), a young
mechanic/Died Mon last, Henry Smith, in the 20th year of his age, son of
widow Smith, near this town. Two children have been removed from this world
in two months; yet the mother found much consolation/Married Tues evening
last by Rev J. Winter, Abraham Koontz to Miss Christiana K..mmer, both of
this co

455. RGM Nov 24 1821/Died at his res near Taney-Town Tues 6th inst after a
lingering illness, James Drummond, in the 52d year of his age/Died Wed 21st
inst after a protrated illness, near Charlestown, Va, where he had removed
only a few months since, Leonard Jamison, for many yrs a citizen of this
co/Died Sat last, Conrad Kellar, old inhabitant of this co and pious Christian

456. RGM Dec 1 1821/Died Sat last, Mrs. Mary Fout, consort of B. Fout, in
the 34th year of her age, leaving husband and 6 children; remains deposited
in Luth burying ground; Mr. Schaeffer delivered discourse/Died suddenly Wed
night last, Augustus Kellog, stranger; remains deposited in English Presby
burial ground, attended by Rev P. Davidson

457. RGM Dec 8 1821/Married Thurs evening last by Rev J. Winter, Shadrack
Larue to Miss Rebecca Wayman, both of Fred. co/Died Thurs 22d ult, Mrs.
Rebecca Ogle, old widow lady of this place/Died Tues morning last, John
Bruner, miller, of this co/Died at his res in Cambridge, Dorch co, 22d ult,
Benjamin W. Lecompte, Esq. in the 36th year of his age

458. RGM Dec 29 1821/Married Thurs last by Rev Schaeffer, John Eholt to
Miss Mary Remsburg, all of this co/Died in this town Wed night last, Dr. G.
J. Schneider, native of Germany, who lately emigrated to this country;
possessed uncommon abilities as a surgeon and physician; a great part of his
life was spent in active military service in the late wars of Europe; and
the wounds which he received in the army rendered him very infirm and
subject ot frequent attacks of sickness

459. RGM Jan 5 1822/Married Sun evening last by Rev Davidson, Aquilla Tally
to Mrs. Gleson/Married Thurs last by Rev David F. Schaeffer, Jacob Starget
to Miss Mary Michael, all of this co/Married same day by Rev J. Winter,
Joshua Davis to Miss Anne Lewis, all of this co

460. RGM Jan 12 1822/Married Tues last by Rev Helfenstein, Valentine Adams
to Miss Sevilla Thomas, all of this co/Marrried same day at Emittsburg by
Rev Dubois, Alexander H. Jarboe, to Miss Teresa A. Grover, all of Frederick
Co/Married Thurs evening 10th inst by Rev Alfred Griffith, Enoch Beall to
Miss Susan Bowhoen(?), both of Liberty/Married Tues evening 8 inst by Rev
Alfred Griffin, Rev Dennis H. Bartie to Miss Elizabeth Jones, dau of Rev
Joshua Jones, all of this co/Married Thurs last by Rev D. F. Shaeffer,
Edward Trail to Miss Lydia Remsberg, both of this city

461. RGM Feb 9 1822/Died after a long and painful illness in Wheeling, Va,
Thurs 31 ult, Col. John Houston, in 62d year, formerly of this place/Died 26
ult, Upton S. Reid, esq. of this co

462. RGM Mar 2 1822/Married Sun last by Rev J. Winter, John Kurtz to Miss Margaret Hargate, both of this co/Married Thurs last by Rev D. F Schaeffer, Daniel Batzold to Miss Margaret Rap, both of this co

463. RGM Mar 9 1822/Died Fri 1st inst, William Housz, in 91st year of his age

464. RGM Mar 16 1822/Married Thurs evening last by Rev D. F. Schaeffer, Samuel B. Bager to Miss Elizabeth Smith, both of this co

465. RGM Mar 23 1822/Died Sat last, aged 55 yrs, George Cox of this city /Died same day, Mrs. Wagoner, aged (?) yrs (number ends in "2"), consort of Upton Wagoner, of this city

466. RGM Apr 6 1822/Married Sun last by Rev Schaeffer, Daniel Stub to Miss Elizabeth Widrick, all of this place/Married same day by Rev J. Winter, John Stull to Miss Catharine Widrick, both of this co

467. RGM Apr 13 1822/Died last week, Peter Wissinger, aged 78 yrs/Died, Captain A. Eder, aged 67

468. RGM Apr 20 1822/Died Yesterday morning at 3 o'clock, John Whittingdon/Married in New Market Sun evening 7th inst by Rev James L. Higgins, Joseph Evitt to Miss Margaret Ann Nichols, both of this co/Married Sun last by Rev Schaeffer, Joseph Umpage, to Miss Eliza Russell of this co/Married Thurs last by Rev Schaeffer, Samuel Houpt to Miss Harriot Atkins all of this co/Married same day by Rev Davidson Rev Samuel Knox, formerly principal of the Frederick Academy, and lately Pres of the Balt College, to Miss Zeruiah McCleery of Frederick

469. RGM Apr 27 1822/Married Sun last by Rev Schaeffer, Michael Winpigler, to Miss Elizabeth Goodman, all of this co/Married Thurs last by same, John Shipman to Miss Miranda Fischer, all of this city

470. RGM May 4 1822/Married Tues 16th ult by Rev Wm. Armstrong, Dr. Samuel Turner, of Loudon co, Va, to Miss Amanda M. Williams, of Mont co, Md/Married Thurs 25th ult by Rev P. Davidson, Elie Groff to Miss Amanda Figgs, all of this co/Died Thurs last in 45th year of his age, Henry Nurz, after a severe and lingering illness/Died same day, Mr. Reed of this place, aged 55 yrs

471. RGM May 11 1822/Reward offered for John Peltz, about 20 yrs of age, apprentice boy of Jacob Leab

472. RGM May 18 1822/Married Sun evening last by Rev Schaeffer, Adam Newport to Miss Margaret Kelly, all of this city

473. RGM May 25 1822/Married Sun evening 12th inst, by Rev Helfenstein, Thomas Doll, to Miss Caroline Kolb, all of this city/Married Sun evening last by Rev Martin, Rudolph Keller, to Miss Elizabeth Hooper, all of this co/Married Tues evening last, by Rev Schaeffer, George Gardner to Miss Hannah Getzendanner, all of this city/Married Thurs last by Rev Schaeffer,

George Whip to Miss Sarah Barnet, all of this co/Died Wed night last, after a short illness, Andrew Thomson, brewer of this city

474. RGM Jun 1 1822/Married by Rev J. Winter, Michael Swigert to Miss Nancy Berry, both of this city

475. RGM Jun 8 1822/Married Thurs evening last by Rev J. Winter, Jacob Reese to Miss Catherine Derr, both of this co/Died 26th inst at his seat near Georgetown, in the 66th year of his age, General Henry Carberry, distinguished officer of the Rev. In that struggle he received a severe wound in the side from a musket ball which could not be extracted without endangering his life

476. RGM Jun 15 1822/Married at Shepherd's Town, Va 5th inst, Edward Bell, Editor of the Virginia Monitor to Miss Catharine Ealy(?)

477. RGM Jun 29 1822/Married Sun 23d inst by Rev Winter, John Casper Frederick to Miss Mary Frieze, both of this co/Married Tues 25th by same, Thomas Weller, to Miss Sophia Stokes, both of this co

478. RGM Jul 20 1822/Died Wed 17th inst Mrs. Lyon, consort of Dr. Isaac Lyon of this place

479. RGM Aug 3 1822/Died Mon last, Jacob Thompson of this co, after an illness of a few days/Died Tues last in Buckey's Town, Reuben Shadwell, native of England

480. RGM Aug 17 1822/Died Wed night last Thomas Young/Married by Rev Schaeffer on 6th inst, Baltzer Fout to Miss Charlotte Kephart, all of this co - on the 8th by same, John Fadely to Miss Catherine Fry - on same day by same, Jacob Jacobs to Miss Anna Vanfossen, all of this co

481. RGM Sep 14 1822/Married Thurs last by Rev Schaeffer, Solomon Kites, to Miss Sarah Grim/Died Tued evening last, Independent, son of John Hughes, Esq., aged 2 yrs, 5 months, 5 days, after an illness of only 30 hrs, with convulsive fits, occasioned by the worms/Died 9th inst, Henry Getzendanner, aged 48 yrs, 2 months, 28 days; he labored under a pulmonary affliction/Died 9 inst George Zimmerman, son of Michael Zimmerman in the 14th year of his age

482. RGM Sep 21 1822/Married Sun last by Rev J. Winter, George Martin to Miss Catharine Hawn, both of this co/Married Thurs last by Rev Schaeffer, Jacob Pfleiderer to Miss Elizabeth Wagner

483. RGM Sep 28 1822/Married Sun last by Rev J. Winter, George Smith to Miss Catharine Biston, both of this co/Married by Rev Schaeffer, John F. Wolbert to Miss Christiana Focht, all of this city/Married Tues last by same, Abdiel E. Magers, to Miss Ruth Philips, all of this co/Died in Washington City on 17th inst, Mrs. Hannah Polkinhorn, after an illness of 12 days; she had been married a fortnight/Died in Balt on 20th inst after a short illness, James Beachem, Printer, aged 22 yrs/Died Sun night last, Jehu Chandler, editor of the Maryland Republican, in the 38th year of his age,

native of Delaware but resided in this city during the last 13 yrs of his life.

484. RGM Oct 19 1822/Died on 2d in the 19th year of her age, Mrs. Eliza Chandler of Annapolis; in the same fortnight the husband and wife descended to the tomb.

485. RGM Oct 26 1822/Married Thurs last by Rev Schaeffer, William Biggs to Miss Ann Hatten, all of this city

486. RGM Nov 2 1822/Died at an early hour last Wed morning, Mrs. Maria Rebecca Ebert, wife of John Ebert, esq. of Frederick

487. RGM Nov 9 1822/Died Tues last in the 75(?)th year of his age, David Sholtz, res of this city

488. RGM Nov 16 1822/Died - Major M'Glassin, lately appointed U.S. factory in the Arkansas Territory, in the place of Mathew Lyon, decd

489. RGM Nov 23 1822/Married Thurs evening 14th inst by Rev Davidson, William T. Davis to Miss Mary Shire, all of Frederick co/Died Thurs last in 81st year of his age, Martin Waltz, of this co. He resided a number of yrs in this place in which he settled about 50 yrs ago and became very useful in the capacity of a carpenter; purchased a farm on which he resided until his death

490. RGM Nov 30 1822/Married Sun last by Rev Schaeffer, William Carter to Miss Frances Nolan, both of Loudon co, Va/Married same day William Eder, to Miss Jemima Boocher, all of this co/Married in Balt on Tues evening 19th inst, Rev Robert Elliot of Washington, D. C. to Elizabeth dau of late Daniel Lammott, Esq of Balt/Married Tues evening 12th inst at George Town, D. C. by Rev Balch, Henry Upperman, sen., aged 80 yrs, to Miss Margaret Gibbs, aged 65 yrs, all of that place

491. RGM Dec 7 1822/Married Fri 29th ult by Rev McElroy, William R. Stitchberry, late of New York, to Mrs. Dorthea Shafer, widow of capt. Conrad Shafer, late of this place

492. RGM Dec 14 1822/Died yesterday afternoon, Joseph Flemming, in the 60th year of his age

493. RGM Dec 21 1822/Married Sun last by Rev McElroy, Micha (spelled Micah in New Citizen) Keepers to Mrs. Susan Stevens, all of this co/Married Tues last by same, Samuel Kessler, to Miss Mary Ann Stonebraker, all of this co/Died Wed last, after a long and lingering illness, John J. Ott, of this co, aged 68 yrs

494. RGM Dec 28 1822/Died Sat evening last, Mrs. Elizabeth Drill wife of Andrew Drill and dau of Capt. Michael Hauser/Also same evening, Mrs. Drill wife of Christian Drill

495. RGM Jan 4 1823/Died Mon last, Mrs. Jones, at an advanced age, occasioned by her clothes catching fire while busied about the hearth; native of North Wales, leaving a numerous family, a husband and several grand children - Balt Patriot.

496. RGM Feb 1 1823/Died Mon morning last, after a short but severe illness, in the 20th year of his age, Frederick S. Nelson, son of late gen. Roger Nelson of this City/Died Thurs morning last, Mrs. Bantz, wife of Henry Bantz, Senr. of this place

497. RJGM Feb 8 1823/Married 30th ult by Rev J. Winter, Benjamin Biggs, to Miss Delilah Graff, both of this co/Married Thurs last by Rev Helfenstein, Gabriel Thomas to Miss Mary Magdaline Harget, all of this co/Married Tues last by Rev Zadwick, William S. Hays, to Miss Eleanor Hardy, both of Barnesville/Married same day Emanuel Ebbert of this city, to Mrs. Wood of Emmittsburg

498. RGM Mar 8 1823/Married Sun evening last by Rev McElroy, Edward Koontz, to Miss Rebecca Lilly, all of this place/Married at Balt, Mr. F. G. Ringgold, to Miss Ann Bradshaw - Mr. E. W. Pratt to Miss Catharine Ringgold - William Ringgold to Miss Rebecca Ringgold and William Ringgold of Easton to Miss Mary R. Ringgold/Died 2nd inst Mrs. Mary G. Hammond, consort of John Hammond /Died Sat 22nd ult, Henry Graff, aged 64 yrs of big Pipe Creek, Fred. Co

499. RGM Apr 5 1823/Married Thurs last by Rev John Winter, William Fitler (Filler?) to Miss Rebecca Link, both of this co/Died Mon last, Benjamin Hagan/Died in Phila on 30th ult in 67th year of his age, George Krebs(?)

500. RGM Apr 12 1823/Married Tues last by Rev D. F. Schaeffer, John Snyder to Miss Mary Whip/Married Thurs last by same, Jacob B. Haller(?) to Miss Elizabeth M. Bash - Hiram Reese to Miss Lydia Carr - M. Daniel Seirg to Miss Barbara Hankey

501. RGM Apr 26 1823/A little boy named George Kennedy, was drowned on Monday last, in Carroll's Creek - Citizen.

502. RGM May 3 1823/Married Mon evening last by Rev McElroy, Madison Nelson, Esq. to Miss Josephine Marcilly, all of this city/Died Sat morning last, John William Miller in the 84th year of his age, of this city

503. RGM May 10 1823/Married Tues night last by Rev P. Davidson, William C.. Smallwood, to Miss Rosana Rollington, all of this city/Married Tues evening last by Rev D. F. Schaeffer, Joseph B. Webb to Miss Mary Foggil(?), all of this city/Married Thurs evening last by same, Jacob Layman to Miss Sevilla Freshour, all of this co/Died on 3d inst on Merryland Tract, Jacob Shoots, after an illness of 10 months

504. RGM May 31 1823/Married Sun last by Rev Schaeffer, Adam Halbrunner, to Miss Eliza M. Crabbs

505. RGM Jun 7 1823/Married Sun last by Rev D. F. Schaeffer, Henry Repp, to Miss Christiana Finkbone, all of this co

506. RGM Jun 21 1823/Married Tues last by Rev D. F. Schaeffer, Jacob Shotts to Miss Rebecca Sultzer, all of this co/Died Mon night near this city, Franklin, son of J. Hughes, Esq.

507. RGM Jul 28 1823/Married Tues evening last by Rev D. F. Schaeffer, Adam Stull, jr. to Miss Margaret Zimmerman, all of this co/Married same day by Rev McElroy, John Wright to Mrs. Young, widow of late Thos. Young, all of this city/Died Thurs night, 12th inst at Woodsborough, after a lingering illness of two yrs, Mrs. Minerva D. Towne

508. RGM Jul 26 1823/Alexander Duvall, who shot major N. Musgrove his father in law, on 6th inst, in Mont co, was taken on Tues following and it is said is now in jail in Washington. Major Musgrove was an officer in the rev army and at the time of his death could have been but little short of 70 yrs of age

509. RGM Aug 2 1823/Died last Wed, Miss Sophia Harriet Krugh, dau of Rev. J. Krugh, remembered by people of Frederick. His dau, the deca, was for some yrs much afflicted; she died from an attack of the palsy

510. RGM Aug 9 1823/Died yesterday morning, Miss Sophia Brunner, dau of late Jacob Brunner, of this place/Another Rev Officer gone. Maj. Cornelious H. Mills is no more, upward of 40 yrs the Serg't of Arms to house of delegates of this state.

511. RGM Aug 16 1823/Married Tues last by Rev Scheffer, John Wachter of Samuel to Miss Sophia Dottero, all of this co/Married Thurs last by Rev Schaeffer, Solomon Burner, to Miss Elizabeth Link, dau of Thomas Link, all of this co

512. RGM Aug 23 1823/Married Tues evening last by Rev D. F. Schaeffer, David Michael to Miss Elizabeth Fout, dau of late Wm. Fout

513. RGM Aug 30 1823/Married Thurs last, 28 inst by Rev Schaeffer, Joseph King to Miss Margaret Houck, all of this co

514. RGM Sep 6 1823/Married Tues last by Rev D. F. Schaeffer, Thomas Ott to Miss Mary Sinn, all of this city/Died Tues last, Mrs. Miriam Campbell, consort of Randolph Campbell, of this co

515. RGM Sep 13 1823/Married Thurs evening 4 inst by Rev J. Helfenstein, Jacob Knouff to Miss Deborah Phillips, all of this co/Died Thurs 4 inst, John A. Schawacker, old inhabitant of Frederick

516. RGM Sep 20 1823/Married Tues evening last by Rev D. F. Schaeffer, Jacob Atkinson of Carlisle, Pa, to Miss Sarah Kitro, of this co/Died Sat last, Frederick Shelly, of this place/Died Sun evening last, Mrs. Barbara Rutherford, old inhabitant of this town

517. RGM Sep 27 1823/Married Tues last by Rev D. F. Schaeffer, John Heffner to Miss Mary Houck, both of this co

518. RGM Oct 4 1823/Died Thurs evening 25 ult in 43d year, Mrs. Mary Houck, consort of John Houck/Died Tues morning last, after a severe and lingering illness, Thomas Conner, of this place/Died in City of Washington 25 ult, after an illness of 10 days, Rev Louis R. Fechtig, elder in M.E. Church and Presiding Elder of Balt District at time of his death

519. RGM Oct 11 1823/Died at Shepherd's Town, Va, Tues last, after a short illness, James S. Lane of that place, enterprising and wealthy merchant/Died 7 inst in Shepherd's town, Va, Miss Margaret C. Shutt, dau of Philip Shutt of that place - Harpers Ferry Free Press

520. RGM Oct 18 1823/Died at Harrisburgh, Pa, 8 inst, Mrs. Mary S. Snyder, consort of late Gov. Snyder, aged 55/Died at Hagers-town, morning of 29 ult, after a short illness, Job Hunt, formerly a res of this city, in 39th year of his age - Balt. Patriot

522. RGM Oct 25 1823/Married Tues last by Rev D. F. Schaeffer, Peter Thomas to Miss Susan Whip, all of this co/Married Thurs evening 16 inst, Camden R. Nichols to Miss Margaretta Phillips dau of Capt. Levi Philips, both of Hyatt's town, Mont Co/Died Sat last at house of Reaser & McCulley, John K. Rest, native of Loudon Co, Va; interred at English Presby Church/Died last on Mon evening, very suddenly at Middleburg, James Neale, Esq., formerly a res of this city/Died a few days ago in this city, after a long state of suffering, Philip Loveder, a native of England/Died in George-Town, D.C., Tues last, Augustus B. Taney, Esq./Died at Deerfield, Portage, Co, Ohio, 24 ult, Mrs. Day, wife of Col. Day, aged 69, occasioned by a sting of a yellow wasp, while she was drying apples and survived but 15 minutes

523. RGM Nov 1 1823/Married Thurs evening last by Rev D. F. Schaeffer, Enos Schell to Mrs. Charlotte Beatty, all of this place/Died Tues night last, Henry Zealer, aged inhabitant of this co/Died same day, Thomas, infant son of John Rigney, Esq./Died Tues night last, David, infant son of Samuel Webster

524. RGM Nov 8 1823/Died lately at New Orleans, Henry T. Beatty, esq. Editor of New Orleans Iris and son of Dr. C.A. Beatty of George-Town, D.C.

525. RGM Nov 15 1823/Married Tues last by Rev Whaeter, George Layman to Miss Mary Stimmell, all of this co/From Torchlight - Died Fri night last in 23d year, Miss Matilda Gruber dau of John Gruber of this place of lingering consumption, interred German Reformed Church burying ground; sermon given by Rev Reily

526. RGM Jan 3 1824/Married Sun evening last by Rev McElroy, John Tehen (Tshen?) of Harpers' Ferry, Va, to Miss Catharine Carlin, of that city

527. RGM Jan 10 1824/Married 22 ult by Rev Schaeffer, George Gavyre to Miss Sophia Heckman(?), all of this city/Died 31 ult in 84th year of her age, Mrs. Mary Wright, relict of Joseph Wright, of this co

528. RGM Jan 24 1824/Married Thurs evening last by Rev Helfenstein, Jacob Myers to Miss Christena Newens/Married lately, Peregrine Mantz, formerly of this city, to Miss Nancy Miller, of Wythe Co, Va

529. RGM Jan 31 1824/Married Tues 20 inst by Rev Beverly Waugh, Washington Burgess, son of late Capt. Burgess, to Miss Mary Ann Stier of New-Market

530. RGM Feb 7 1824/Married Tues 13 ult by Rev Greer, Doctor Samuel Annan of Emmittsburg to Miss Mary Jane, eldest dau of John M'Kaleb, Esq. of Taney-Town/Died 7 ult at his res on the Potomac, Samuel Luckett, in the 53d year /Died 13 ult, Warner, infant son of Lewis Birely of that town/Died in city of Washington, 19 ult, John Erskine, Printer, aged about 40 yrs

531. RGM Mar 6 1824/Married Tues by Rev Schaeffer, Richard Anderson to Miss Susan Riggs, all of this co/Married Thurs last by Rev Schaeffer, John Whip to Miss Margaret Thomas, all of this co

532. RGM Mar 13 1824/Married Sun last by Rev D. F. Schaeffer, John Schaeffer to Miss Susanna Widdel

533. RGM Mar 20 1824/Married Thurs last by Rev Schaeffer, Abraham Earnest, to Miss Barbara Earnest, all of this co

534. RGM Jan 12 1826/Married Thurs 22d ult by Rev Matthews, Dr. William Waters of this city, to Miss Frances Conway, dau of Col. James Hite, of Jefferson co, Va./Died 12th ult at res of her son-in-law, John Getzendanner, Mrs. Elizabeth Hoffman, long a res of this co, having attained to fourscore yrs/Died at Georgetown, D.C. Tues 27th ult of consumption, David Haller, formerly of this city, in the 23d year of his age/Died 28th ult at the res of her husband, Mrs. Mary Cockey, consort of the Hon. Joshua Cockey, Senator of this state/Died Sun morning 1 Jan, Mrs. Nancy Biggs of this city/Died 9 inst, after a short illness, Conrad R. Kolb

535. RGM Feb 9 1826/Married Sun evening last by Rev D. F. Schaeffer, George Eader to Miss Catharine Derr, all of this city/Married same day by same, Samuel Shook, to Miss Susannah Rice, all of this co/Died Wed evening 1st inst, Lewis Green, of this city, in prime of life/Died in neighborhood of Fred'k, Mon evening last, Mrs. Myers, widow of the late Christian Myers, in the 81st year of her age/Died Sun morning last, Christian Scholl, old and respectable inhabitant of this vicinity/Another Sage of the revolution gone! David Shriver, senior, died Sun night, 25 ult, near Westminister, in 91st year of his age

536. RGM Jun 1 1826/Married Thurs 9 inst in Hartford co, Master Lee Amos, aged 15 yrs, to Miss Mary Roberts, aged 22 yrs/Died Tues 9th ult, Mrs. Elizabeth Norris in the 77th year of her age, for many years an inhabitant of this place

POLITICAL EXAMINER & PUBLIC ADVERTISER

Published by S. Barnes, Market Street, Frederick Town

537. PEM Feb 2 1820/Married last evening by Rev Johns, John Buskirk to Miss Lucinda Grahame, both of Loudon Co, Va

538. PEM Mar 22 1820/Married last evening by Rev Hammond, Zebulon Kuhn, Esq., to Miss Amy, dau of Jacob Biggs, Esq., all of this co

539. PEM Mar 29 1820/Married Mon evening 27 inst by Rev James Lee Higgins, Dr. John Hammond McAlfresh to Miss Theresia Mantz, dau of Francis Mantz, all of this co

540. PEM May 10 1820/Married Thurs 27 ult by Rev Gieger, Francis Mathias to Miss Nancy, dau of Joshua Cocky, Esq., all of this co/Married Thurs evening last by Rev Jonathan Helfenstein, John L. Levy to Miss Ann Louisa Hauser, all of this place/Married same evening by Rev Schaeffer, Michael Sultzer to Miss Mahala Thomas, all of this place

541. PEM May 17 1820/Shocking Death - Fri last, Col. James S. Hook of this co whilst examining his saw-mill, accidently stept on some loose plank, which giving way, he was precipitated amonst the wheels and machinery, and instantly crushed to death/Died Sat last at Boonsborough, Capt. Abraham Lamastre, age 78 yrs; buried with masonic honors/Married last evening by rev Maleve, Ethelbert Taney to Miss Elizabeth M. Jarboe, all of this co/Married in Cumberland 4 inst, Samuel Magill, Esq., Post-master, to Miss Emma, dau of John Whitehead, all of that place

542. PEM May 31 1820/Died a few days ago, Adam Baer, inhabitant of city of Washington, formerly a res of this city. He was on board a small vessel on the Potomac and was knocked over board by the boom and drowned

543. PEM Jun 28 1820/Married Thurs evening 15 inst by Rev J. Helfenstein, George Buckey, Esq., to Mrs. Mary Cook, all of Frederick Co/Married Thurs evening last by rev Armstrong, Festus Dickinson, Esq. of Va, to Elizabeth dau of Capt Brashear of Frederick Co

544. PEM Aug 30 1820/ Peter M'Kiernan in Frederick Town offers reward for apprentice to plastering business, Lloyd Cumpton, 19-20 yrs of age, 5 ft 6-7 inches, slender made

545. PEM Sep 6 1820/Married Sun evening last by Rev Maleve, John Flaherty to Miss Rebecca T. Winnull, all of this town

546. PEM Nov 1 1820/Married Sun evening last by rev John Grobp, Abraham Lynn to Miss Eve Schwartz, both of Taney-Town

547. PEM Nov 29 1820/Samuel Webster offers reward for apprentice David Reynolds, about 19 yrs of age

548. PEM Dec 6 1820/Died Friday 1st inst, of pulmonary disease, in the 26th year of his age, James Wright of this place/David Luckinsland offers reward

of 6 cents and half a dozen thrumbs for apprentice to weaving business, James Ship, age about 17, about 5 ft, 2 inches

549. PEM Feb 9 1825/Died 1 Feb at house of Miss Tarbot in Westiminster, Susan Bruce Scott, in the 19th year of her age, eldest dau of John Scott of Pipe Creek; gentle and retiring in her disposition/Died at Elkton Mon evening 17th ult, Philip Harding, esq., cashier of Elkton bank; formerly res in Frederick Co.

550. PEM Apr 18 1827/Married at Liberty-town Tues evening last by Rev Nicholas Snethen, Capt. James C. Atlee of New Windsor (Sulphur Springs) to Miss Sarah S. Jones dau of Abraham Jones, Esq. of the former place

551. PEM Jun 6 1827/Married Sun evening last by Rev Shane, Lloyd M. Norris, merchant, to Miss Elmira M., eldest dau of Jesse Cloud, Esq., all of Balt

552. PEM Aug 1 1827/Married Thurs last by Rev Walsh, Joseph Jamison, to Miss Martha Ann Combs, all of this co/Married same day by Rev McElroy, Michael Crough to Miss Rosanna dau of late Thomas Conner of this city.

553. PEM Aug 15 1827/Married Thurs 2d inst by Rev S. Helfenstein, William Mahn to Miss Susan Hilderbrand, both of this co

554. PEM Nov 21 1827/Died Mon morning last, after a short illness, Charles Kellar of this town

REPUBLICAN CITIZEN & STATE ADVERTISER

By G. W. Sharp, Westminster, Maryland. Also called New Citizen.

555. NCM Aug 31 1821/Died Wed morning last, Joseph, little son of Anthony Arnold of Balt Co

556. NCM Sep 21 1821/Now published in Frederick, Md. - Married Thurs evening 6 inst by Rev Maleve, David Young to Miss Margaret Jones, all of this city/Married Sun evening 9 inst, John Stouffel to Miss Nancy Skinner, all of this co/Died Wed 12 inst, Jacob Smith, aged 23 yrs/Died at York, Pa, Thurs 6 inst, after an illness of a few days, Henry Faust, Printer, in the 20th year of his age - York Recorder.

557. NCM Sep 28 1821/Died Mon 17 inst at Hanover, Pa, Miss Susannah Forney, dau of M. David Forney of Balt. She was on a visit to her relations in this place, after a confinement of 2 weeks - from a lingering pulmonary complaint of 6 yrs - Hanover Guardian.

558. NCM Oct 5 1821/Died Tues 25 ult, Jane Beall, dau of Elisha Beall, of this co/Died Sun morning last, John Doll of this city, in the 46th year of his age/Died Wed morning last, Peter Bruner, aged inhabitant of this co/Died yesterday, Jacob Malambre of this city/Died recently in Phila, George Helmbold, ed. of Independent Balance

559. NCM Oct 12 1821/Died in Union-town, Md., Mrs. Mary Bentley, consort of Isaac Bentley and eldest dau of George Harbach of that place, in the 25th year of her age/Died Thurs morning 4 inst, Capt. John Burgess after an illness of 2 weeks/Died Mon last, Catharine School, consort of John Scholl of this co, in the 46th year of her age/Died Tues last, Adam Snook of this co in the 71st year of his age/Died Wed 3d, Miss Susannah Smith, in the 59th year of her age/Died recently at Lancaster, Pa, George Price, ed. of Free Press

560. NCM Oct 26 1821/Died Mon night, 22 inst in this city, Dr. Edward R. Eastburn son of Robison Eastburn, Esq. of this co, in the 20th year of his age/Died lately at Westminster, Mrs. Magdalena Brown, wife of John Brown of that place, for some time afflicted with a painfull illness/Died 18 inst after an illnes of 10 days, John Woodrow, Esq., Mathematician and formerly Surveryor of this co, aged about 70 yrs/Died near New Windsor in this co, 13th ult, John Ecker, in the 76th year of his age

561. NCM Nov 9 1821/Died Wed 31 ult, Miss Mary Carlin of this city, in the 26th year of her age, after an illness of 3 weeks; remains deposited in the Cath cemetery/Died Wed evening last by an apoplectic fit, John Ramsberg, esq., of this co/Died 3d inst, William Birley

562. NCM Nov 16 1821/Died Sat last, 10 inst, at New Market, Francis D. Wayman, of this co, in the 24th year of his age

563. NCM Nov 23 1821/Equity case - Edward Richards & Jane his wife, Sarah Davidson, James Death & Anne his wife, John Root, Edward Riley & Ann his wife, George Crowl & Margaret his wife, Hugh M'Clunn & Mary his wife, Henry Greer & Elizabeth his wife, Philip Hines & Lydia his wife, John Cook & Sarah his wife, Ann Taylor, David Root, Daniel Root of James, John Poution & Elizabeth his wife, Nathan England & Harriet his wife - to sell real estate of Margaret Root, decd, Frederick Co, who died intestate. Complainants and defendants are her heirs at law. Of these persons the following reside out of the state of Md.: Edward Richards & Jane his wife, Sarah Davidson, James Death & Anne his wife, John Root, Edward Riley & ann his wife, George Crowl & Margaret his wife, Hugh M'Clunn & Mary his wife, Henry Greer & Elizabeth his wife, Philip Hines & Lydia his wife, Daniel Root of James, John Poution & Elizabeth his wife, Nathan England & Harriet his wife

564. NCM Dec 14 1821/Monday evening last an old man named Claude Jolley who kept store in S. Charles St., Balt, was murdered and his store robbed of about $1000 of goods

565. NCM Dec 21 1821/Married Sun evening 9 inst by Rev D. F. Schaeffer, Jacob Riehl to Miss Catharine Boswell, all of this city/Married Thurs 13 inst by same, George Blessing to Miss Susan Easterday, all of Frederick Co/Married Thurs 29 ult by Rev Thomas G. Allen, Dr. William M. B. Willson of this place to Miss Martha Wooton of Mont Co, Md/Died Mon 10 inst after a tedious illness, Mrs. Catharine Widrick in the 75th year of her age/Died Wed 12 inst, Mrs. Susanna Biggs, after a long and tedious illness, in the 42d year of her age/Died suddenly Wed 12 inst, Gen. Richard K. Heath of 14th

Brigade of Maryland Militia. He participated in the defense of Balt in 1814.

566. NCM Dec 28 1821/Married in this city Wed evening last by Rev Helfinstein, Daniel Hiram to Miss Maria Potts, both of Loudoun Co, Va/Died Wed night in this city, Dr. G. J. Schneider; funeral from house of Mrs. Sheffer in Market St.

567. NCM Jan 4 1822/Married at Balt Mon 24 ult by Rev A. Helfenstein, Dr. John Baltzell of Frederick to Miss Ruth, youngest dau of late Charles Ridgely of William/Married Tues 25 ult in City of Lancaster, William Albright, Editor of Americanische Staatsbothe to Mary Weaver, both of that city

568. NCM Jan 11 1822/Reward offered for negro Frank who calls himself Francis Hill about 27 yrs of age, 5 ft 4-6 inches - by Lloyd Luckett near New Town (Trap)

569. NCM Feb 1 1822/Married in this city Sun evening last, Laurence Doyle to Miss Sarah Gordan (spelled Gordon in the Examiner)/Died Fri 18 inst after a lingering illness, Mrs. Sarah Magers, consort of Greenberry Magers, esq. of this co, in the 58th year of her age, leaving husband, son and 2 daus /Died Sat 19 ult, Richard Colegate, in 76th year of his age/Died Sun evening last in this city, Mrs. Magdalena Sheffy, in the 83rd year of her age

570. NCM Feb 8 1822/Married Thurs 31st ult at Green Castle, Pa, by Rev James Buchanan, Daniel Kemp to Miss Hariet Eliza, dau of Christian Kemp, Esq. of this co

571. NCM Feb 15 1822/Died Fri last after a few days illness, Miss Susan Kemp dau of Col. Henry Kemp of this vicinity, in the 15th year of her age /Died at Annapolis Sat 2d inst, James Brook, Esq., delegate to General Assembly for Kent Co, in 57th year of his age/Died in Wheeling, Va, 31st ult, Col. John Houston, formerly of this place/Died Fri morning last, Jonas Whitmore, res of this co/Died Sun evening last, Thomas Hoffman of this city, in 29th year of his age

572. NCM Mar 15 1822/Died Mar 8, Thurs last, George Martz, in the 70th year of his age/Died Fri last, John Shaneholtz, in 25th year of his age/Died same day, William Housy and Tues last after a short illness Jacob Brunner of this city in 63d year of his age/Equity case - Mary Debruder by her next friend vs James Debruder, Lewis Medtart & Henry Nixdroff - to obtain decree in favor of Mary Debruder for property left to her by her late father, Jacob Medtart. She married James Debruder around 1801 and lived with him about 2 yrs. During that time said Debruder pursued a very ruinous and intemperate course of life and thereby reduced his family to a state of extreme poverty; he abandoned said Mary Debruder and her infant dau about 17 yrs ago and migrated to some part of the Western Country. About 10 yrs ago said Debruder married a woman in the state of Ohio and continues to live with her. Complainant prays that the court will direct Lewis Medtart and Henry Nixdroff, exec of Jacob Medtart to secure the property to her use

573. NCM Mar 22 1822/Died recently near Westminster, Francis Adelsperger

/Died at his res near Westminster a few days ago, Andrew Reese, aged inhabitant of this co

574. NCM Apr 19 1822/(portion of paper missing)/Married Wed 10 inst by Rev David Martin, Samuel Pearl to Miss Catharine Houck, of this co/Married Tues 9 inst by Rev Shaeffer, David Cramer, to Miss Martha Scholl, eldest dau of John Scholl, Esq./Married Thurs 11 inst by Rev Shaeffer, George Snouffer to Miss Eliza Raneberger, all of this co/Married Sun last 14th by Rev Shaeffer, Joseph Umbrage to Miss Elizabeth Russel, both of Loudon Co, Va

575. NCM Apr 26 1822/Died Wed 17 inst in Creagers-town, Henry McDonnell, in 28th year of his age, leaving 4 sisters and 3 brothers

576. NCM May 3 1822/Married Thurs 18 ult by Rev Schaeffer, Samuel Houpt to Miss Harriot Atkins, all of this co

577. NCM May 10 1822/Died Thurs 2nd inst, in the 45th year of her age, Henry Nusz, after a severe illness

578. NCM May 24 1822/Married Sun evening by Rev Martin, Rudolph Keller to Miss Elizabeth Hooper, all of this co/Died Wed night last of a short illness, Andrew Thompson, brewer, of this city, husband and father

579. NCM Jun 14 1822/Equity case - Henry Weller & Catharine his wife and Barbara Shover vs. William Kishwood & Julia his wife, Catharine Shover and Elizabeth Shover and others - for sale of tract, Buck's Forrest in Frederick Co, 137 acres, property of Sophia Shover, decd, who made her will before she came into possession of said tract. She died 8 May 1822. She had 4 children: (1) Sophia (wife of Daniel Rouzer) who is dead leaving children; (2) Sinor who is likewise decd, leaving 4 children, viz. Julia (wife of William Kishwood), Jacob Shover, Adam Shover, Catharine Shover & Elizabeth Shover; (3) Catharine (wife of Henry Weller) and (4) Barbara Shover; the complainants in this behalf.   William Kishwood & Julia his wife, Catharine Shover and Elizabeth Shover res out of state of Md. [There are inconsistencies in the above stated relationships.   Original court records should be consulted.]

580. NCM Jul 5 1822/Kidnappping - My child, a boy of 8 yrs of age was stolen, when at play near his home in Frederick Co, 26 May last, by it is supposed a man named John Wolford. My child is well grown and very black; his name is Solomon and calls himself Solomon Humant. John Wolford is about 5 ft 10 inch, stout, pock marked, a part of his nose has been bitten off, about 40 yrs of age. He was confined some time ago in the penitentiary at Balt - William Humbere, laborer (free man) at Catoctin Furnace/Reward offers for negro man Luke Adams, 27, about 5 ft 11 inch, Samuel Adams about 37, 5 ft 10-11 inch - William I. Johnson near Barnesville, Mont Co

581. NCM Jul 12 1822/Died Sat 29 ult in Hanover, Pa, after a severe and painful illness, Adam Forney, tanner, aged 68 yrs, 14 days; interred in burying ground of German Ref. Church of this place - Hanover Guardian/Married in Balt by Rev Gray, Dr. James Bain to Miss Mary Ann Donnelly/Died at Westminster Sun Jul 7th, Jacob Sherman, Esq., aged 66 yrs

582. NCM Jul 26 1822/Equity case - Mary Souder, Peter Souder, Antony Souder, Michael Souder, Elizabeth Souder and Margaret Souder vs. John Cost and Richard Cost and others - for sale of real estate of Philip Souder, decd, in Frederick Co, who died intestate about 24 Sep 1820, possessing several tracts of 325 acres. Heirs of Philip Souder: Mary Souder, Peter Souder, Anthony Souder, Michael Souder, Elizabeth Souder, Margaret Souder, Rachel wife of John Cost, John Souder and Margaret Cooper. John Cost and Rachel Cost res in Ohio

583. NCM Aug 2 1822/Michael C. Adelsberger, Emmitsburg, offers reward for apprentice to coopering trade, John Lowry, 19-20 yurs of age, black hair, black eyes and fresh complexion, about 5 ft 9-10 inch. When intoxicated he is free spoken

584. NCM Dec 27 1822/Equity case - Levin West vs. James Rice administrator of estate of Leonard Scaggs, Sarah A. Scaggs and others - for sale of real estate of Leonard Scaggs, decd, who died intestate about 4 Oct 1821. His heirs: Mahala wife of George Winpigler, Elizabeth, Anne, Eleanor, Rebecca, Leonard, Thomas, Sarah, Benjamin, Juliana, Henry, Alexander and John Levin Scaggs. Letter of administration given to James Rice. Sarah Ann Scaggs res in Ohio/Equity case - George Buckey & Marion his wife, Jacob Houck & Catharine his wife vs. Jacob Low, John Low, Jno. Griar & Sarah his wife - for sale of parts of 2 lots in Frederick Town of Andrew Low who died intestate leaving following children at the time: Jacob Low, Marion Low since m to Geo. Buckey and two of the complainants, Catharine wife of Jacob Houck, being the other two complainants. John Low who moved to Va where he died intestate leaving a widow named Sarah who has since m John Griar and sons named John Low and Cyrus Low. Cyrus Low, said Jacob Low, John Griar, and Sarah his wife, and her son John Low an infant, all res out of the state. Cyrus Low died many yrs since, intestate, when an infant.

585. NCM Jan 24 1823/Allegany Co Equity Case - Joseph France agnst Jonathan Clarke & Catharine his wife, John Jonas, William Jonas, Samuel Jonas, John Jonas son of Adolph, Jeremiah Jonas, Elizabeth Jonas, George Jonas, William Barker & Anne his wife, Joseph Everly & Hannah his wife, George Inks & Elizabeth his wife and John Cummens & Lucy Anne his wife - to obtain conveyance for 2 lots westward of Fort Cumberland. Complainant purchased from John Jonas senr late of Allegany Co, decd, said lots who died intestate leaving defendants as heirs. Residing out of state of Md.: Jonathan Clarke & Catharine his wife, John Jonas, William Jonas, Samuel Jonas, John Jonas son of Adolph, Jeremiah Jonas, Elizabeth Jonas, George Jonas, William Barker & Anne his wife, Joseph Everly & Hannah his wife, George Inks & Elizabeth his wife. Under age of 21: John Jonas son of Adolph, Jeremiah Jonas, Elizabeth Jonas, George Jonas.

586. NCM Feb 7 1823/Nicholas Turbutt to leave Frederick Town on or before 1 April; seeks payment of bills owed when he kept tavern

587. NCM Feb 14 1823/Married Tues evening 11 inst by Rev M'Elroy, George Lee of Washington City to Miss Margaret Himmell of this city

588. NCM Nov 4 1825/Equity case - Jacob Everhart acting exec of estate of Jacob Wallman senr vs Ignatius Jarboe, Horatio Jarboe and others - for sale of real estate of Francis Jarboe who died intestate and left heirs, some of whom res out of state

589. NCM Aug 11 1826/Married 3d inst by Rev John McElroy, William Haley to Miss Bridget Fitzpatrick, all of this co/Married Sun evening last by Rev J. Helfenstein, Valentine Albaugh to Miss Rebecca Brunnre, both of this co/Married 8 inst by Rev John McElroy, James Hook to Miss Catharine Jamieson, all of this co

590. NCM Dec 15 1826/Died Sun last, Mrs. Pool, consort of Henry Pool of this town/Died Mon morning last, William Reeves of this town

591. NCM Mar 16 1827/Married Thurs last by Rev D. F. Schaeffer, John P. Gear to Miss Susan Specht, all of this co/Married Thurs 8th at York, Pa, by Rev Dr. Schmucker, Dr. Sherer of Dillsburg to Miss Eliza Eichelberger, dau of Jacob Eichelberger, Esq. of York, Pa/Died Sat evening, Mrs. Catharine Kreblo, of this city, in 61st year of her age after a very severe illness.

592. NCM Mar 23 1827/Married 15 inst by Rev D. F. Schaeffer, Jacob Michael to Miss Catharine Stein, both of this co/Married same evening by same, George Rice, jr., to Miss Henrietta Trager, both of this city

593. NCM Mar 30 1827/Married Thurs evening 22d inst by Rev D. F. Schaeffer, William Small of Balt, to Miss Henrietta Norris of this city

594. NCM Apr 13 1827/Married Thurs 5th inst by Rev F. Stier, Charles H. Shanks to Miss Maria Talbott, all of this co

595. NCM May 4 1827/Died Fri 27 ult after a short illness at his res in Middletown-Valley, Robinson Eastburn, Esq. in the 64th year of his age/Chancery case - Thomas Edmondson vs. Moses B. Farquhar and William P. Farquhar - to rectify alleged mistake in conveyance of land from defendant to complainant. That Moses B. Farquhar sold to complainant lands in Frederick Co, whereof he was res, including part of "Forrest in Need," which had been willed by his father William Farquhar sen. Moses Farquhar resides in Ohio.

596. NCM Apr 11 1828/Died Sat last, Mrs. Catharine Myers, member of Luth Church and who 60 yrs ago assisted the masons in building the old church of this place, aged 79 yrs/Died at his res near Barnesville, Mont Co, Sun last, very suddenly, John Pool, sen., old inhabitant of that co/Died at his res in Washington City after a tedious confinement, Dr. William Thornton, one of the oldest inhabitants of that city, for many yrs head of patent office

597. NCM Jul 4 1828/G. Koontz offers 6 cents reward for mulatto apprentice, William Hammond, 16-17 yrs of age, about 5 ft 1-2 inches, straight hair, fair complexion

598. NCM Jul 11 1828/Married Tues evening 1st inst by Rev D. F. Schaeffer, John Rutter to Miss Henrietta Mayburry, all of this co

599. NCM Nov 7 1828/Married 21 ult by Rev Bosler, Thomas Waltzman to Miss Catharine Wolfe, both of this co/Died Sat morning, John Jestice, in the 25th year of his age/Died Fri Mon last at his farm on Pipe Creek, Henry Kinze, of the Dunker Society, in the 87th year of his age

600. NCM Jun 26 1829/Equity Case - Lingan Boteler vs. Henry Philpott, Charles H. Philpott and others - to convey undivided moriety of real estate of Barton Philpott senr which was bequeathed to Samuel Philpott, decd, by will of his father said Barton Philpott, senr. Barton Philpott sen, died some yrs since, possessed of tract and by his will bequeathed portion to his widow Barbara Philpott during her natural life and after her death to his sons, John Philpott and Samuel Philpott. Barbara Philpott died 4 March 1828. Samuel Philpott died many yrs since, before death of said Barbara, leaving a widow Henny Philpott and 2 children, Charles Higdon Philpott and Ann Catharine Ellen Philpott, all of whom do not res in Md., living in Ky. Children are under age of 21. Also involved is Francis Hamilton who sold all property obtained from will to Lingan Boteler. Francis Hamilton died in 1822 leaving widow and several children among whom is dau Susan Hamilton who m William Keller and resides in Va.

601. NCM Dec 17 1830/Married in Balt 7 inst by Rev Johns, Dr. Thomas W. Johnston of Frederick Co to Eleonora Dalrymple dau of late Alexander Claggett of Balt/Died in Washington City Fri morning last, Mrs. Caroline Kuhn wife of Capt. Joseph L. Kuhn, of U.S. Marine corps/Died Sun 5 inst after a few hrs of illness, Miss Margaret Sinn, wife of Henry Sinn and dau of Nicholas Brengle, of this co

TRUE AMERICAN & FARMERS REGISTER (Rockville)

602. TFL May 28 1824/Died Mon morning at 1 o'clock, General William H. Winder, in the 49 year of his age

603. TFL Jun 4 1824/Married Thurs evening 27th of May last by Rev Green, Thomas Hall to Miss Rebecca Piles, all of Mont Co

THE MARYLAND JOURNAL (Rockville)

604. MJL Vol. 1, No. 1, Thurs Aug 4 1825/Married Thurs 28th ult by Rev Armstrong, John H. Beall, Esq. to Miss Louisa C. Darn, dau of William Darn, Esq. all of Mont Co/Married same evening by Rev Nathan Holland, Isaiah Easton, to Miss Charlotte Haney, all of Mont Co/Mont Co Court case - Edward Waggoner and Zeuriah his wife, A. C. Magruder, George W. Kiger, and George Orrick, vs. Harvey Lane, Hardage Lane, Ninian Edwards and Elvira, his wife; Juliet Swearengen, --- Bridings and Catharine his wife, William H. Lane, William Coleman and Lydia his wife. Object of bill is to obtain sale of tracts which were the property of Samuel Lane, decd. (Although not stated, the defendants are probably heirs of Samuel Lane, decd. - F.E.W.) Harvey Lane, Hardage Lane, Ninian Edward, and Elvira, his wife, Juliet Swearengen, ---Bridings and Catharine his wife, William H. Lane, William Coleman and

THE MARYLAND JOURNAL (Rockville)

Lydia his wife, are all non-residents and beyond the reach of the process of this court/Equity case - Adam Robb vs. Benjamin Pelly, James Pelly, William Pelly, Nathan Pelly, Solomon Pelly, Elizabeth Pelly. Object is to obtain conveyance of title which they derived from Harrison Pelly, Frederick Co, decd, to tract called Wickham's Chance, by virtue of agreement made by Harrison Pelly with John Tucker.

605. MJL Aug 11 1825/Died Sat last, a few miles from this place, Miss Ruth Pumphrey, aged about 23 yrs, dau of Samuel Pumphrey of this co (apparently about to be married)/Hagerstown Aug 2, Wed morning last, Joseph Resh, Sen. put an end to his existence by cutting his throat with a razor. He was a landholder, in easy circumstances, and resided about 6 miles from this place, near Conococheague Creek, and not far from the residence of Capt. John Wolgamot in this co. We have been informed that the free use of ardent spirits was the principal cause of the unfortunate man's untimely end - he having indulged the idea that himself and family were tormented with witches. &c. He has left a large and distressed family

606. MJL Sep 8 1825/Died in this village, 22 ult, son of Leonard Howard, aged 17 months/Died in vicinity of this place, 25 ult, Barton Harris, aged about 50 yrs/Died in this co, 27 ult, William Holmes, aged nearly 70/Married Mon 5th inst by Rev Duvos, Lloyd F. Harding to Miss Mary Ann Knott, all of Mont Co/Married Tues 6 inst by Rev Thomas Green, Jonathan Browning to Miss Polly Hobbs, all of Mont Co

607. MJL Sep 15 1825/Married Sun evening 10 inst, by Rev Armstrong, John T. Viers, to Miss Eleanor Reid, all of this co/Died near Rockville, Mon 12th inst. James Ryan, aged about 62 yrs/Died 10th inst in Alms House of this co, Sarah Gates, aged about 80 yrs

608. MJL Sep 29 1825/Married Thurs 20th inst by Rev J. B. Magruder, Rev Walter Cross of Annapolis, to Miss Sarah Holland, dau of Rev Nathan Holland, Jun. of this co/Married Tues 27th inst by Rev ---, Willson Lewis to Miss Rebecca Harper, all of Mont Co

609. MJL Oct 11 1825/Died Wed night last, after a short but severe illness, Esther Riley, wife of Rev Tobias Riley of Mont circuit, in the 32nd year of her age

610. MJL Oct 18 1825/Married Tues evening last by Rev Mines, Grafton Hammond of Frederick Co, to Miss Mary Elizabeth Ann Rebecca Wilson, dau of Thomas Wilson, Esq. of this place/Married Thurs last by Rev John Magruder, Henry Wright of Frederick Co, to Miss Sarah Burrows, of Mont Co

611. MJL Oct 25 1825/Married in this place Thurs last by Rev Thos. G. Allen, John Flemming of George Town, to Miss Ann Coberth, of Mont Co

612. MJL Nov 1 1825/Married Sun evening 23d ult. at Winchester, Va, Col. Thomas Plater, of this co, to Miss Elizabeth Buchanan, dau of late Pinckney Buchanan of Frederick Co/Married Sun last by Rev Devoust, Thomas N. Clements, to Miss Lydia Ann Livers, all of Mont Co

613. MJL Nov 8 1825/Married Tues evening last by Rev Thomas G. Allen, Thomas Griffith, to Miss Elizabeth Griffith, dau of Col. Lyde Griffith of this co /Married same evening in Brookville, by same, Wm. J. Dorsey, to Miss Susan R. Robertson/Died in Annapolis, Md., Sun morning last, in the 19th year of her age, Miss Elizabeth Watts, dau of Richard B. Watts

614. MJL Nov 15 1825/Married Thurs 3d inst by rev Grust, John H. King, merchant of George Town, D. C. to Miss Ellen, dau of late Elias Harriott, decd, of Carlisle, Pa/Died at Fredericktown Tues morning last, William Thomas, son of Dr. Wm. M. B. Willson, aged about 3 yrs/Died Sat evening last, with the croup, after a few hours illness, Thomas Gassaway Perry, son of Elbert Perry, aged 5 yrs

615. MJL Nov 22 1825/Married Thurs evening last by Rev Thomas G. Allen, Nathan Cook, to Miss Elizabeth Magruder, all of this co/Died at Pensacola, Florida, 23 Sep, George F. Brent, formerly of Va; on his death bed, just a few hours before he died, he married Miss Merced A. Gonzalez by Rev Maenhaut of the Cath Church, of which they were both members

616. MJL Nov 29 1825/Married Thurs 24th inst by Rev ---, Wesley Duley to Miss Eliza Dove, all of this co

617. MJL Dec 1825/Married Thurs last by Rev Joseph H. Jones, Alfred Clagett, of Wash Co, to Miss Susan M. Clagett of Mont co

618. MJL Dec 20 1825/Married Tues last by Rev Watters, William White to Miss Ann Fletchall, all of this co/Married at New Haven Mon evening, 5th inst by Rev Croswell, Joseph H. Bradley, Esq. of this co, to Miss Lucy A. Tuttle, dau of Asahel Tuttle, Esq. of the former place

619. MJL Dec 27 1825/Married Wed evening last at the city of Washington, by rev David Baker, Jeremiah Gettings, of Pa, to Miss Serine O. Scott of Mont Co

620. MJL Jan 24 1826/Married Thurs evening last, at Darnestown, by Rev John B. Magruder, Magruder Bell, to Miss Mary Ann, eldest dau of John Candler, Esq./Married same evening at the same place by Rev John Mines, James Offutt, to Miss Rosannah Elenor, 2nd dau of John Candler, Esq. all of Mont Co/Married this evening near Poolsville, by Rev Thomas G. Allen, Elisha W. Williams, to Miss Jane Plater, dau of Thomas Plater, esq. all of this co

621. MJL Feb 7 1826/Died 21st ult in the vicinity of this place, Mrs. Nancy Joy, wife of Enoch Joy, aged about 35 yrs. The decd went to bed apparently in health, and in the course of the night was found dead by her husband/Died suddenly on the 31st ult, Mrs. Precilla Nicholls, wife of Major Thomas C. Nicholls of this co, aged about 43 yrs

622. MJL Feb 21 1826/Married Mon evening last by Rev Mines, Thomas J. Dewan, to Miss Eliza Sufton, both of Va/Married Thurs evening last by Rev Chapman, John S. Harding, to Miss Martha Browning, both of this co /Died this morning, Mrs. Rachael Gettings, of the prevaling epedemic, consort of Berry Gettings, of this co

THE MARYLAND JOURNAL (Rockville)

623. MJL Feb 28 1826/Died 15th inst, John Thomas, in the neighborhood of Sandy Spring, aged 92 yrs

624. MJL Mar 7 1826/Married Thus last by Rev Thomas G. Allen, James Windham, to Miss Mary Riley, all of this co

625. MJL Mar 14 1826/Married Tues evening last by Rev Joseph H. Jones, Otho Saffell, to Miss Amelia Ann Merrick, all of this co/Married Thurs last by Rev ---, Jesse Seberns, to Miss Elizabeth Sands/Married same evening by Rev John Mines, Dennis Moulden, to Miss Serah Ann O'Neal, all of this co

626. MJL Mar 21 1826/Died Sat last in this co, Erasmus Perry, aged 66 yrs, taken suddenly after breakfast that morning and died in the evening/Married Thurs evening last by Rev J. Mines, Enoch Joy, to Mrs. Elizabeth Harriss, all of Mont Co

627. MJL Apr 4 1826/Married Thurs evening last by Rev J. B. Magruder, Robert Ricketts, Printer, to Miss Rachel Moulding, both of Mont Co/Married Thurs last by Rev Thomas G. Allen, Solomon Lemon, to Miss Eleanor Manan, both of this co/Married Tues in Zion Church, Frederick Co, by Rev John Johns, Rev William Armstrong, Jr., Rector of said church, to Miss Eliza Johnson, dau of Major Roger Johnson of said co/Married in Washington City, Thurs morning last by Rev Hawley, Michael Connelly, to Mrs. Drusilla Nicholls, both of Mont Co/Died 24th ult, Mrs. Penneloper Brown, aged about 80 yrs, of this co

628. MJL Apr 18 1826/Married at Fredericktown Thurs evening, 6th inst by Rev Jonathan Helfenstien, Charles Nagle, editor of the Political Intelligencer or Republican Gazette, to Miss Sophia Rollington/Died in this co 30th ult, John B. Magruder, aged about 83 yrs/Died a few days since, Washington Bowie, aged about 50 yrs/Died Fri 14th inst in Rockville, at his residence, John A. T. Kilgour, Esq. 31 yrs of age, able lawyer and advocate; his corpse taken to the Episc Church where the Rev T. G. Allen delivered a discourse /Sat last William Leech, who was on his way to George Town, with a team belonging to Jacob Reed, of Frederick co, in attempting to get off the saddle horse (at the lower end of this town) his foot hung fast in the stirrup, and threw him under the wagon, and the fore wheel of the wagon passed over his left arm and breast. He died in about 8 hours afterwards. His remains were on Monday removed to Fredericktown by his employer, for interment. The decd has his back broke some year back, by a wagon running over him, and it is said that this has been the fourth wagon that has run over him

629. MJL Apr 25 1826/Married Thurs evening last by Rev John B. Magruder, Gassaway Watkins, of Balt, to Miss Catherine Willett, of this co/Married Sun last, at Triadelphia Factory, by Rev ---, William Webb, to Miss Hannah Phealen, all of this co

630. MJL May 2 1826/Another Rev Hero gone! Died at his residence in Liberty-Town, Mon evening 14 Nov last, Major General Robert Cumming, commander of the first division of Md. Militia, in the 72d year of his age. Address delivered by Rev Caleb Reynolds

THE MARYLAND JOURNAL (Rockville)

631. MJL May 16 1826/Married Thurs last by Rev Plummer Waters, Charles King to Miss Agnes Beall, all of Mont Co

632. MJL May 30 1826/Died Fri morning 12 inst, at his residence near Damascus in this co, James Norwood, aged about 59 yrs

633. MJL Jun 6 1826/Married 22nd ult by Rev Devos, Edward Gaffney, to Miss Elenor Ryan, all of this co/Married 25th ult by Rev ---, Berry Griffith, to Miss Sarah Tilly, all of this co/Married 1st inst by Rev Thomas W. Green, George Reid, to Miss Elizabeth Smith, all of this co

634. MJL Jun 20 1826/Married Tues 23d ult at Barnesville, by Rev Chapman, John Simmons of Frederick Co, to Miss Martha E. Tillard of this co

635. MJL Jun 27 1826/Married Thurs evening last by Rev T. G. Allen, John Poole, jr. to Miss Sarah Dickerson, dau of Nathan Dickerson, both of this co

636. MJL Nov 7 1826/Married Thurs 26 Oct by Rev Joseph H. Jones, Thomas W. Riggs, to Miss Elizabeth Northcraft, all of this co/Married Sun 22d ult at his father's residence, Anne Arundle co, by Rev Linthicum, Henry H. Forsyth, merchant of Cracklintown, Mont Co, to Miss Polly Dorsey, of the former co

637. MJL Dec 26 1826/Married Thurs last near Darnes-town, by Rev Thos. G. Allen, Otho Boswell, to Miss Margaret Connelly, all of this co/Married Thurs 14th inst near Barnesville, by Rev Thomas Green, William Jones, to Miss A. A. Hodges, all of Mont Co/Died at her mother's residence, in the vicinity of this place, Mon last, Mrs. Martha Willson, wife of Dr. Wm. M. B. Willson, of Frederick Town, aged 25 yrs and 3 days, leaving husband and several children, one of which is only about 9 weeks old

638. MJL Oct 10 1827/Chancery case - Cordelia V. B. Magruder, and others vs Thomas Bowie and others. Subject of this bill is to have suit and proceedings revived and to put in the same plight and condition as they were in before the death of Upton Beall, one of the complainants, and Washington Bowie, one of the defendants. The bill states that in March 1824, Cordelia V. B. Magruder, Ellen B. Magruder, Richard H. Griffith and Upton Beall, exhibited their bill of complaint aginst Washington Bowie, Dr. John Bowie, Henry Griffith of Lyde and Eliza his wife as the defendants, praying that certain lands should be sold for the payment of certin single bills and that Dr. John Bowie might be sustained from prosecuting any suit agnst said Upton Beall and Richard H. Griffith, upon two single held by Eliza V. Magruder, which had been paid by and assigned to said Dr. John Bowie as is set forth ...said suit afterwards abated by the death of Dr. Bowie and a bill of revivor was filed agnst the said Hy. Griffith & wife & said Washington Bowie of Montgomery Co, Thomas Davis and wife and Thomas Bowie, Humphrey B. Bowie, Washington Bowie, and Richard Bowie of Prince George's Co, heirs of said Dr. Bowie. Before the process of the court was served the proceeding became abated by the death of Washington Bowie, of Montgomery Co and Upton Beall. Washington Bowie left Thomas J. Bowie, Washington Bowie, Richard J. Bowie, Robert G. Bowie, Margaret Bowie and Mary Chichester, who m George M. Chichester and resides in the state of Va, his heirs at law. Upton Beall by his last will appointed Adam Robb his executor/Married in this place Tues

last by Rev Thomas G. Allen, Edward A. Gantt, Esq. of Frederick Co, to Miss Kitty Ann Anderson, dau of Dr. James Anderson of this place/Died Sun last after a short illness, at Clarksburg, Rev Caleb Reynalds, for many yrs a traveling Meth Preacher

THE MARYLAND JOURNAL AND TRUE AMERICAN (Rockville)

639. MJL Wed, Jan 2 1828/Married Tues evening 1st inst by Rev J. H. Jones, Hilleary Piles, to Miss Matilda Bruner, both of this co/Married Sun evening last by Rev J. H. Jones, Levi B. Pennifield to Miss Margaret Hill, both of Mont co

640. MJL Jan 9 1828/Married Thurs last by Rev Thomas G. Allen, Charles Saffell, jr., to Miss Elizabeth M. Thompson, all of this co/Married Tues evening last by Rev Maurus, George H. Graves, merchant of Barnesville, Mont co, to Miss Elizabeth Stone, of Balt

641. MJL Jan 16 1828/Died at his res near Hyatt's-town Sun 6th inst, Archibald Nichols, aged inhabitant of this co, patriot and soldier in the Continental Army

642. MJL Feb 6 1828/Died 18th ult at Barnesville, Mrs. Margaret Muse, consort of Ignatius P. Lyles, Esq., in the 24th year of her age/Died at Middlebrook Mills, Fri, 1 Feb, 1828, at 2 o'clock, A.M., Capt Edward Howes, aged about 68, long an inhabitant of this co

643. MJL Feb 20 1828/Married Sun last by Rev Thomas G. Allen, Benjamin Hinton, to Miss Catherine Pennefille, all of this co

644. MJL Feb 27 1828/Married Thurs evening last by Rev J. H. Jones, Adam Beall, Miss Eleanora Fyffe, both of this co/Married Tues evening 19 inst, by Rev Berkby, John F. Barrett, of this place, to Miss Caroline Margaret Elizabeth, only dau of John Wade of Loudoun co, Va

645. MJL Mar 5 1828/Died Fri morning, 29th Feb, John Tayloe, Esq. aged 56 yrs. His remains will be interred at his late res, Mount Airy, Richmond Co, Va - Nat. Int. of March 1

646. MJL Mar 12 1828/Died in this village on Fri morning last, with apoplexy, Henry Lansdale, old res of this place; he had been very much afflicted with rheumatism for many yrs. He had come from his res about 1 miles from this place on Mon morning, and was struck with prostration of strength, while in his carriage, and only survived until Fri evening, being 5 days after the attack

647. MJL Mar 26 1828/Married last evening in this village, by Rev J. H. Jones, Samuel Pumphery, to Mrs. Mary Campbell, both of this place/Died at his res near Barnesville, Sat 23 Mar, Joseph Harriss, sen. in the 67th year of his age

THE MARYLAND JOURNAL AND TRUE AMERICAN (Rockville)

648. MJL Apr 2 1828/Died at his res near Barnesville, on Lordsday last, very suddenly, John Pool, Sen., Esq. an old inhabitant of this co/Died at his res in F St, after a tedious confinement, by malady, Dr. Wm. Thornton, one of the oldest and most respectble of this Citry, who for many yrs, past, presided at the head of the patent office, in the Department of State. - Nat. Int.

649. MJL May 14 1828/Died on Sabbath last, in Rockville, Miss Rachel Longdon, in the 17th year of her age, scholar in the Rockville Sabbath School; ramainst attended to the grave by officers, teachers, and ascholars of the Sabbath School/Died at the res of her mother, Mrs. Sarah Henderson, Mon 5th inst, at midnight, Miss Constant Comfort Cromwell, aged 21 yrs, 5 months, 15 days (long obit)

650. MJL May 21 1828/Died Sun 11th inst at his res in Annapolis, Hon. Jeremiah Townley Chase, within a few days of the terminatinon of the 80th year of his age

651. MJL Jun 11 1828/Died Sabbath morning last, after an illness of 35 hours, Honore Martin, Esq. in the 70th year of his age. He was a native of France, but had early settled in Rockville and resided in it longer than any other citizen of the place. He had 4 sons and 5 daus; their mother died a few years ago

652. MJL Jun 25 1828/Married Thurs evening last, by Rev J. H. Jones, William Boswell, to Miss Jane Burris, both of this co

653. MJL Jul 9 1828/Died a few days since in this neighborhood, Walter Bailey, aged about 50 yrs. He had been complaining of an obstruction in the passage to the stomach, called oesophagus, which increased, and for some months past the only nourishment he was enabled to receive, was conveyed through tubes into the stomach; ultimately the passage closed and he literally starved to death. He was a great lover of tea and for the last 20 yrs of his life he never wished to take a meal without it, and often would eat the tea leaves /Died last Sun 7 miles above this place, Col. James B. Brooks, aged about 53

654. MJL Jul 23 1828/Died 11th inst, at the res of his father in Mont co, Dr. Thomas I. Davis, in the 22d year of his age

655. MJL Aug 6 1828/Died 9th Jul last, Mrs. Catharine Duley, relict of Jonathan Duley, aged 73 yrs/Died Fri last, William B. Penefill, aged about 35 yrs /Died Sat last, James Willett, eldest son of Burgess Willett/Died Sun last, Benedict H. Duley/Died Mon last Rezin Ricketts, only son of late Capt Benjamin Ricketts

656. MJL Sep 10 1828/Jeremiah Brown gives caution that his wife, Elizabeth Brown, has left his bed and board and he shall pay no debts of her contracting/Died after five weeks illness, at the res of her father, in Mont co, Tues 19 Aug last, Miss Amanda Prather, in the 12th year of her age, dau of William and Elizabeth Prather. In the autumn of 1827 there was a Sabbath

school established at Hopewell, between 2 and 3 miles from her parents, where she became a member at its first formation

657. MJL Sep 24 1828/Died a few days since, in this co, Francis Belmare, aged about 22 yrs/Died in this co, a few days since, Richard Harry, aged about 70

658. MJL Oct 1 1828/Died Thurs last, sep 25, Samuel C. Middleton, son of the widow Ann Middleton, aged 19 yrs/Married Tues 30th Sep by Rev Divose, John Gardner to Miss Ann Clements, dau of Bennett Clements, Esq. all of this co

659. MJL Oct 8 1828/Died monring of 2d inst, near Clarksburg, Mont Co, after a severe illness of 8 days, John Fox, in the 40th year of his age, leaving widow and 3 children

660. MJL Oct 15 1828/Died in Washington, D. C. Thurs 2d inst, after a short but very severe illness, Capt J. M. Speake, long an inhabitant of that city, in the 61st year of his age/Mahlon Kirk, Sandy Spring, Mont Co, offers reward for indented apprentice, Charles Berns, about 19 yrs of age, light complexion

661. MJL Oct 22 1828/Died Sat last at his res in Mont co, Lloyd Adamson, Esq., county surveyor, aged about 40 yrs, after an illness of upwards of 3 weeks

662. MJL Dec 10 1828/Married Tues 25th ult, Martin Wheelan, from the Falls of St. Anthony, Mississippi, to Miss Elizabeth Price, of Unity, in this co; as a youth war roused him from "loves young dream," and carried him to the frontier of Canada to meet an invading foe. The vississitudes of a sol- dier's fortune detained him from the arms of his dearest sixteen yrs, when he performed a journey of 1600 miles on foot to consummate his early vows /Died Thurs last at Thomas Clagett's near this place, Miss Rachel Clagett, aged 35 yrs, dau of Doct. Zachariah Clagett, late of Pleasant Valley, Wash Co, Md., decd/Died Sun night last, in Rockville, Mrs. Moulden, consort of Levi Moulden. She had been long afflicted and has left 3 small children, one of whom an infant

663. MJL Sep 9 1829/Died 8th inst, Mrs. Harriss, consort of William Harris, leaving numerous family of children/Died same day, William Clagett, son of Samuel/Died same day, Mrs. Garrett, consort of Thomas Garrett, leaving a numerous family of children/Died a few days since, Mrs. Walter Magruder, after an affliction of about 12 months/Died also a few days since, two of the Miss Glazes

664. MJL Sep 30 1829/Chancery case – William B. Magruder vs Nathan Magruder and others. Object of the bill is to obtain decree to sell real estate of John B. Magruder, decd, as necessary for payment of his debts. The bill states that John B. Magruder was indebted to the complainant in the sum of $40.75 for medicines and attendance as a physician and died intestate in April 1826. The following are his heirs at law: Nathan Magruder, a brother; Susan Singleton, a sister; Walter Hilleary, a nephew; Elizabeth Wells, a grand niece and Alfred Wells a grand nephew, the children of Rebecca Wells,

THE MARYLAND JOURNAL AND TRUE AMERICAN (Rockville)

with Walter Hilleary aforesaid were children of Elizabeth Hilleary, a second sister of the said intestate; Thomas B. Magruder, a nephew; Clarissa Webb wife of James Webb, and Emma Berry wife of Charles Berry, nieces, the children of Isaac Magruder decd, a second brother of the intestate; Rebecca Owings wife of Christopher Owings a niece and James Turnbull, a nephew, the children of Rebecca Turnbull, decd, a third sister of the intestate; Rebecca Magruder wife of Lewis Magruder, Melinda Hilleary wife of Theodore Hilleary, two nieces and Rector Duval, a nephew of the children of Sarah Duvall, a fourth sister of the intestate; Mary Griffith, wife of Richard Griffith, Ellen B. Magruder, Elizabeth Griffith, wife of Henry Griffith of Lyde, Cordelia R. Griffith wife of Jeff.. Griffith, Matilda Magruder wife of ...er Magruder, nieces, and Jeffry P. Magruder and Lewis Magruder nephews of the children of Jeffry Magruder decd, a third brother of the intestate. Alfred and Elizabeth Wells are infants, under age of 21, and Susan Singleton, Charles Berry and Emma his wife, James Turnbull, Lewis Magruder and Rebecca his wife, Theodore Hilleary and Melinda his wife, and Rector Duvall, reside out of the state of Md

665. MJL Jan 27 1830/Married last evening by Rev J. H. Jones, Ransel Mowyer to Miss Ruth Burriss

666. MJL Sep 15 1830/Died at his res near Middlebrook Mills, Fri 27th Aug last, Zadok Cook, aged 29 yrs/Died in this co, a few days since, Thomas Gassaway, leaving a widow/Died in this co, Mrs. Offutt, wife of Ozgood Offutt, at an advanced age/Died in this village, Sat last, after a long and tedious affliction, William Braddock

667. MJL Nov 10 1830/Died in Balt Tues 3d inst, after a painful illness of more than two weeks, Jane McClenahan, aged about 66 yrs

668. MJL Dec 8 1830/Married Thurs evening last, by Rev L. I. Gillis, James Magruder, Jr. to Miss Elizabeth A. T. Riggs, all of Mont co/Died Thurs morning 2d inst, Thomas Cramphin, at his late res in this co, aged 90 yrs and 10 months/Died a short time past, Joseph Roberts and his brother Wm. Roberts, both of this co

80

INDEX

This is an index to the PARAGRAPH number NOT the page number. Titles
such as Captain, Doctor, Junr., etc., have not been used except when given
names were not in the newspaper item.

...ain George 448
ADAMS James 75; Luke 580; Samuel 580;
  Valentine 460; William 384
ADAMSON Lloyd 661
ADELSBERGER Michael C. 583
ADELSPERGER Francis 573
AGNEW Martha 133
AHULT Jacob 409
ALBAUGH Valentine 589
ALBERT John L. 202
ALBRIGHT William 567
ALLEN Barbara 99; Mary 332; Rev T. G.
  628, 635; Robert 332; Thomas G.
  203, 287, 565, 611, 613, 615, 620,
  624, 627, 637, 638, 640, 643
ALLIX Michael 39
AMOS Lee 536
ANDERS Alexander 332; Esther 332;
  Henry 332; James 332; John 332;
  Margaret 332; Samuel 332
ANDERSON Catherine P. 157; Edward
  157; James 287, 638; Kitty Ann
  287, 638; Richard 531
ANGEL Peter 221
ANNAN Andrew 396; Margaret 312; Mary
  Jane 192; Robert L. 277; Samuel
  133, 192, 530
ANSTONE Henry 85
ARMOUR James U. 411
ARMSTRONG John 3; Rev 91, 100, 183,
  341, 418, 543, 604, 607; Rev W.
  374; William 57, 61, 93, 185, 188,
  221, 285, 330, 470, 627
ARNOLD Anthony 555; Frances Eliza
  134; Joseph 555
ASPER Elizabeth 439
ATKINS Harriot 468, 576
ATKINSON Jacob 516
ATLEE James C. 550
AUCHINCLOSS Matilda 135
AYRES Rebecca D. H. 350

BACON Ann 238; Dr. 238
BAER Adam 17, 542; Elizabeth 337;
  Hannah 452; Henry 321, 337; John
  321, 324; Maria Elizabeth 245;
  Mary 324; Michael S. 146
BAGER Samuel B. 464

BAILEY Walter 653
BAIN James 581
BAKER David 619; Henry 254; Sarah
  290; William 25
BALCH Rev 490
BALTZEL John 429
BALTZELL Ann Mary 364; Catharine 206;
  Charles 206; David 429; Elizabeth
  429; George 429; Jacob 364, 429;
  John 159, 567; Lawrence 429;
  Margaret 429; Mary 429; Michael
  445; Rebecca 429; Samuel 429;
  Susanna 429; Thomas 324; Thomas A.
  324
BANKS Charles 374
BANTZ Elizabeth M. 414; Gideon 414;
  Henry 387, 496; Mrs. 496; Nimrod
  404; William 95
BARKER Anne 585; William 585
BARNET Sarah 473
BARRETT Exile 130; John F. 644
BARTGIS M. E. 255, 263; Matthias 177
BARTIE Dennis H. 460
BASH Elizabeth M. 500
BATZOLD Daniel 462
BAUCHER Lydia 377
BAUGHER Charlotte 180; Frederick 180;
  Joseph 133; Rev 404
BAUSMAN Elizabeth 53; Mary Eliza 381
BAXTER Cormack 90
BEACHEM James 483
BEALL Adam 644; Agnes 631; Elisha 93,
  445, 558; Enoch 460; Harriet 285;
  Jane 558; Jemima Ann 93; John H.
  604; Perry W. 445; Upton 258, 638;
  William Dent 371; William M. 122
BEAM Robert M. 180
BEATTY Charlotte 523; Dr. C. A. 524;
  Henry T. 524; John M. 51; Lewis A.
  26; Sarah 26
BEAUCHAMP William 163
BEAVANS Mary Ann 415
BECHT Joseph 221
BECKBAUGH Magdalena 164
BECKENBAUGH George 295; Lydia Ann
  409; Sophia 92
BEDINGER Daniel 227; Mrs. 227
BELL Edward 476; Magruder 620; Samuel
  446

81

INDEX

Henry 75, 98, 481; Jacob 98; John
210, 534; Jonathan 49; Mary 98
GEYER Rebecca 157
GIBBS Margaret 490
GIBSON Harriet E. 148; Mary 43
GIEGER Rev 540
GILBERT David 384
GILLIS Rev L. I. 668
GIRLLING Rev 318
GIST George W. 2; Independent 399,
447; Joshua 275; Mordecai 447;
Rachel 399; Rev H. 250; Sarah 275
GITTINGS Juliet Ann Caroline 91
GLAZES Miss 663
GLENN Lewis W. 181; William 199
GLESON Mrs. 459
GOLDSBOROUGH Catharine E. W. 291;
Edward Y. 250; Leander W. 394;
William 227, 291
GOMBER Christina 69; Esther 387; John
69, 387
GONZALEZ Merced A. 615
GOODMAN Elizabeth 469
GORDAN Sarah 569
GORDON Sarah 569
GRAAFF Caroline 341; Sebastian 341
GRABILL Henrietta 278
GRAFF Ann C. 2; Delilah 497; Elie 61;
George 229; Henry 135, 498; Mary
196; Sebastian 2, 229
GRAHAM Eliza 308
GRAHAME James 299; Lucinda 537;
Richard 328; Thomas I. 262; Thomas
J. 75
GRAVES George H. 640
GRAY Rev 581
GREAVES Rev 94, 451
GREEN Lewis 214, 535; Rev 603; Thomas
606, 637; Thomas W. 633
GREENWALD Christian 400; Mary
Magdalene 400
GREER Elizabeth 563; Henry 563; Rev
133, 530; Rev R. S. 271, 278
GRIAR John 584; Sarah 584
GRIER Dr. 357; Rev 133; Rev R. S. 312
GRIEVES Mary 182; Thomas 182
GRIFFIN Alfred 460; Rev 28
GRIFFITH Alfred 429, 460; Berry 633;
Cordelia R. 664; Eliza 6838;
Elizabeth 613, 664; Henry 638,
664; Isaac 269; Jeff... 664; Lyde
613, 638, 664; Mary 664; Mr. 137;

Rev 40; Richard 664; Richard H.
638; Samuel 275; Thomas 613
GRIM Sarah 481
GROBP John 546
GROFF Elie 470
GROG Rev 376
GROHP John 37; John G. 356
GROSEMAN Elizabeth 298; Simon 298
GROSS Catharine 241
GROVE Leonard S. 340; Margaret 52;
Susan 309
GROVER Teresa A. 460
GRUBER John 525; Matilda 525
GRUHP John 101
GRUST Rev 614
GUNTON Harriet 43

HADERMAN Mr. C. J. 314
HAFF Frances jane 15
HAGAN Benjamin 499
HAINES Daniel 77
HALBRUNNER Adam 504
HALEY William 589
HALL Baruch 420; Mary 420; Nicholas
36; Notley 228; Thomas 603
HALLER Catharine 284; Darcus 336;
David 210, 534; Jacob B. 500; John
135; Joseph 284; Philip 101, 336
HAMBLETON John 296
HAMILTON Francis 600; Francis A. 397;
Susan 600
HAMMER James G. 410, 420
HAMMOND Charles 23, 300; Eliza 72;
Elizabeth 23, 300; Grafton 200,
610; John 498; Mary G. 498; Nathan
93, 401; Philip 401; Rev 538;
Upton 62; William 597
HANE William 178
HANEY Charlotte 604
HANKEY Barbara 500
HANNA John 328; Martha R. 328
HANSHEW Henry 172; John 242, 375;
Mary 242
HARBACH George 559
HARDESTY Richard M. 384
HARDING Cassandra 186; Elias 186,
309; Eliza H. 77; John L. 9; John
S. 622; Lloyd F. 606; Mary 404;
Philip 168, 549; Roger Johnson
309; Walter 309
HARDT Peter 38
HARDTS Catharine 433

HARDY Eleanor 497
HARGATE Margaret 462
HARGET Mary Magdaline 497
HARGROVE John 85
HARMAN Margaret 343
HARPER Mary 128; Rebecca 608; Richard
128; Robert Goodloe 167
HARRIOTT Elias 614; John 6
HARRIS Barton 606; George C. 333;
John 333; Margaret 333; Matilda
333; Thomas 333; Washington 333;
William 663
HARRISS Elizabeth 626; Joseph 647;
Mrs. 663
HARROTT Ellen 614
HARRY Richard 657
HART Jacob 419; John 207, 398; Mary
120
HARTLEY Tamer 347
HARTMAN Abraham 347
HARTSOCK Pamilia 353
HARTZ Francis 368
HASSELBACH John 236
HASSELBACK Rebecca 374
HATCH William S. 192
HATTEN Ann 485
HAUER Daniel J. 323
HAUGH Henry 255
HAUGHN Adalineah 313
HAUSER Ann Louisa 540; Louisa Hauser
M. 13; Michael 494; William 144
HAWKINS Thomas 40
HAWLEY Rev 10, 627
HAWN Catharine 482
HAYES Joseph 254; Leonard 185;
Matilda 254
HAYS William S. 497
HAYSER William 436
HEATH Richard K. 565
HEBB Edward T. 145; Mary 145
HEBBARD Ebenezer B. 126; William B.
333
HECHMAN Sytha 91
HECKMAN Sophia 527
HEDGE Enos 49
HEDGES Andrew 137; Elizabeth 137;
Joseph 80
HEFFNER John 517
HEICHLER Henry 353
HEINKLE Amelia 200
HELFENSTEIN Albert 399; Catharine
327; Jonathan 45, 49, 51,104, 169,

264, 293, 327, 346, 350, 361, 368,
399, 436, 540, 549, 628; Louisa C.
399; Rev 102, 126, 139, 159, 172,
178, 184, 221, 317, 460, 473, 497,
528; Rev A. 237,567; Rev J. 13,
18, 46, 52, 53, 117, 164, 202,
234, 247, 251, 279, 308, 334, 444,
515, 543, 553,589; Samuel 263, 275
HELFENSTINE Jonathan 222; Samuel 225
HELFINSTEIN Rev 566
HELMBOLD George 558
HEMPSTONE William 57
HENDERSON Robert 219; Sarah 649
HENKLE Harriot S. 218; Moses M. 194
HENSHAW Rev 238, 350
HERRING Caspar 419; Catharine 207;
Mary 419, 451
HERRON Francis 283
HEUGH John 62
HICKEY Rev 133
HICKLEY Rev 396
HICKSON Mary 72
HIGGINS James L. 9, 10, 59, 80, 97,
129, 313, 360, 420, 468; James Lee
539; Rev J. L. 303
HILDERBRAND Susan 553
HILL Christian 298; Francis 568;
Lewis 298; Margaret 298, 639;
Martha 298
HILLEARY Elizabeth 664; Melinda 664;
Theodore 664; Walter 664; William
160
HILTON James 236; Susan G. 404
HIMMELL Margaret 587
HINES Lydia 563; Philip 563
HINTON Benjamin 643
HIRAM Daniel 566
HITE James 210, 534
HITT Daniel 201; Rev 373; Samuel 201
HOBBS Polly 606; Samuel 300; Susan
300; William 300
HODGE Elizabeth 332; Francis 332
HODGES Miss A. A. 637
HOFF Jacob 201; Peter 400
HOFFMAN Ann M. 45; Elizabeth 210,
534; Francis 446; George 309;
George W. 421; John 45; John
Hamilton 309; Mrs. 446; Rev J. N.
223; Thomas 571; William 269;
Wilson 153
HOLFENSTEIN Rev 120
HOLL John 448

INDEX

664; Rev J. B. 627; Rev J. G. 608; Robert P. 72; Thomas B. 664; Walter 663; William B. 664
MAHN William 553
MAIN John 429
MALAMBRE Jacob 558
MALAVE Francis 78; Rev 11, 428, 433, 442, 445, 541, 545, 556
MALLAVE Rev 77
MANAN Eleanor 627
MANTZ Ann 451; Charlotte 20, 192; Christianna E. 380; David 229; Eleanor 9; Ezra 315; Francis 9, 20, 103, 442, 539; Henry 342; Isaac 192, 213, 451; John 374; Peregreine 528; Peter 229; Susan 374; Theresia 9, 539
MARCILLY Josephine 502
MARCKEY Frederick 51
MARECHAL Most Rev Ambrose 301
MARESCHAL Most Rev Archbishop 206
MARESHAL Most Rev Archbishop 228
MARKELL Jacob 217, 311; Rebecca 311
MARKEY Frederick 282, 434
MARSH Joel 27
MARSHALL Richard H. 104
MARTIN David 20, 219, 224, 353, 358, 393, 397, 418, 574; George 482; Honore 651; Jacob 422; Luther 234; Rev 157, 177, 178, 203, 206, 269, 473, 578; Rev D. 286
MARTZ George 572
MATHEWS Rev 210
MATHIAS Francis 540; Peter 1
MATTHEWS Jesse 42; Rev 295, 534
MATTHIAS John 285
MAURUS Rev 640
MAYBURRY Henrietta 598
MAYNARD Ephraim H. 10; George W. 97
MAYNER Elijah 332; Nancy 332
McALFRESH John Hammond 539
McCAIN Rev 61
McCANN Michael 269
McCAULEY John 161; Rev 309
McCLANAGHAN Michael 423; Susan 423
McCLEERY William 423; Zeruiah 468
McCLENAHAN Jane 667
McCLERY Robert 423
McCULLOUGH John W. 355
McDADE Samuel 198, 439
McDONNELL Henry 575
McDUELL Henry 404

McELFRESH Ariana 276; Henry 276
McELROY John 589; Rev 122, 130, 161, 491, 493, 498, 502, 507, 526, 552
McGILL Elenor 340; Patrick 340
McGUIRE Miss R. A. 271
McKIERNAN Peter 442
McLEAN Daniel 223
McNEAL John 256; Mary 256
McNIEL Amelia 163
McPHERSON Alexander 216; Col. J. 267; Edward B. 251; John 126, 437; Sarah 437
McVICKAR William 198
MEALEY Francis Thomas 360
MEASEL Joseph 375
MEDART Jacob 432
MEDTART Jacob 50, 572; Lewis 572
MELTZHEIMER Rev 180
MERCER Cornelius 379; John F. 446; Joshua 310
MEREDITH J. 404; Jonathan 306; Mary 51; Rebecca 306; Thomas 51
MERING George 390
MERRICK Amelia Ann 625
MERRITT Samuel 127
MESSLER John 248; Margaret 248
METCALFE Basil 124
METZGAR Jacob 430
MICHAEL David 512; Jacob 592; Mary 459; William 335
MIDDLETON Robert White 318; Samuel C. 658
MIERS Sophia 109; William H. 71, 109
MILLER Benjamin M. 101, 417; Caroline 351; Charlotte 159; Daniel 84; Edward 414; Elizabeth 196; John 281; John S. 320; John William 502; Mrs. 41; Nancy 528; Rebecca 217; Rebecca Catharine 320; Samuel 159; Sarah Ann 417
MILLS Cornelious H. 510; Mary Ann E. 377; Richard 95
MINES John 620, 625; Rev 200, 610, 622; Rev J. 626
MINOR John 201; Mary Berkely 201
MISCIMMINS Abraham 196; Israel 196; James 196; John 196; Rachel 196; William 196
MOBBERLY Dr. E. W. 247
MOBLEY Levi 224
MOCKABOY Sopus 430

INDEX

MOORE Alfred L. 286; Daniel M. 19;
Hannah 332; John 332; Thomas 166
MORELAND John 339
MORGAN John 329; Selina Amelia 194;
William V. 194, 371
MORRIS Elizabeth 43; James 43; John
G. 314; Rev 323
MORRISON Alexander 332; James 226,
268; Jane 226; Rev 342; Sarah 332
MOSS Mary Ann 388
MOTTER Ann M. 309; Eliza 396; George
440; Joshua 218; Lewis 309, 353,
396
MOULDEN Dennis 625; Levi 662; Mrs.
662
MOULDING Rachel 627
MOWYER Ransel 665
MUHLENBURG Henry 55
MULLIKAN Ann 420; James 420
MURDOCH Benjamin 164; Eleanor 329;
George 15, 229, 329; Mary C. 15;
Matilda 164; Richard B. 183;
William 183
MURPHY James 164
MURRAY Lydia 264
MUSATER Anna Maria 96
MUSE Margaret 642
MUSGROVE Major N. 508
MYERS Catharine 308, 596; Christian
215, 535; Eliza 454; Elizabeth
172; Jacob 528; John 138; Mary
172; Michael 171; Miranda 380; Mr.
R. 172; Mrs. 215, 535; Rudolph 172

NAGLE Charles 222, 628
NAYLOR Mahala 251
NEALE James 522
NEFF Mary 453
NEIDIG Benjamin 237
NEIGHBOURS Elizabeth R. 268
NEIGHHOFF Gabriel 223
NEILL Alexander 144; Rebecca 144;
Thomas 144
NELSON Burgess 264; Emmaline 168;
Frederick S. 496; Henry 180;
Madison 502; Nathan 168; Rev 6;
Roger 496
NEVINS Rev 125; William 306
NEWENS Christena 528
NEWPORT Adam 472
NICHOLLS Drusilla 627; Precilla 621;
Thomas C. 621

NICHOLS Ann H. 202; Archibald 641;
Camden R. 522; George 415; James
271; Margaret Ann 59, 468; Seth
353
NICODEMUS Abraham 172; Andrew 395;
Elizabeth A. 395; Philip 395;
Washington 395
NIDIG Abraham 295; Ann 295
NIXDORFF Samuel 137
NIXDROFF Henry 572
NOKES Richard 114
NOLAN Frances 490
NORMAN Mary Matilda 314
NORRIS Basil 30, 84; Deborah 313;
Elizabeth 30, 536; Henrietta 593;
John 114; John D. 342; Jonathan
342; Lloyd M. 551; Margaret 28;
William 251
NORTHCRAFT Elizabeth 636
NORWOOD James 230, 632
NURZ Henry 470
NUSZ Cyrus 309; Henry 577

O'NEAL John 382; Serah Ann 625;
Susanna 382
O'NEILL Catherine 96
OFFUTT James 620; Mrs. 666; Ozgood
666
OGLE Elie 6; Rebecca 457
OLLIX Adam 428
ORR Esther 332; Robert 332
ORRICK George 604
ORTNER Caroline 27
OTT George 13; Jacob 13; John J. 493;
John William 423; Mary C. 423;
Michael 265; Thomas 514
OWENS Theodore 236
OWINGS Christopher 664; Patrick 287;
Rebecca 664; Zebulon 287

PADGETT Mr. A. 403
PARAGRAFT Jane 332; Jonathan 332
PARKER William 10
PARKS Margaret 224
PATTERSON Ann 429; Jane 396; Nancy
40; Rev 6
PAXTON Samuel 332; William 332
PAYNE Eleanor 27
PEARL Samuel 574
PEARRE Alexander 170; James 198;
Tabitha 170
PECK Benjamin 381; Caroline 381

93

TALBOTT Ann 251; Joseph 251; Maria
  594
TALLY Aquilla 459
TANEY Augustus 41, 121; Augustus B.
  522; Ethelbert 541; Harriott 6;
  Jane 37; Joseph 6; Octavious 37;
  R. B. 402
TARBOT Miss 549
TAYLOE John 645
TAYLOR Ann 563; John Wesley 314
TEASER Hetty 183
TEHEN John 526
THOMAS Catharine 178; Charles C. 73;
  Eleanor 66; Elias 298; Elizabeth
  192; Emanuel 398; Gabriel 192,
  335, 497; Henry 178, 335; John 66,
  73, 100, 101, 623; John Hanson
  231; Lloyd 99; Mahala 540;
  Margaret 531; Mary Ann 39; Mary C.
  100; Peter 522; Raleigh Colston
  231; Richard 244; Sevilla 460;
  Susanna(h) 4, 269; William 614
THOMPSON Andrew 578; Charles 288;
  Elizabeth M. 640; Jacob 479;
  Michael 246
THOMSON Andrew 65, 106, 161, 473;
  Charles 152; Grace 241; John 161;
  Margaret P. 302; William C. 412;
  William J. 393
THORNTON William 307, 596, 648
TICE Henry N. 361; Margaret 151
TIERNAN Ann Elizabeth 206; Luke 206
TILGHMAN George 224
TILLARD Martha E. 634
TILLY Sarah 633
TING Rev 102
TISE Margaret 435
TOBERRY Elizabeth 184
TODD Charles W. 384
TORMEY Patrick 183
TORRANCE Ann 420; James 75, 420;
  Rebecca Ann L. 75
TOW Lucinda 283
TOWNE Minerva D. 507
TOWNSEND Sarah 263
TRAGER Henrietta 592
TRAIL Amanda 330; Edward 460; William
  330
TRISLER George 245, 287, 436;
  Henrietta 436; Margaret 308;
  Rosanna 245
TRUNDLE Ann V. 57

TSHEN John 526
TUCKER Jemima 430; John 604
TURBUTT Maria 240; Nicholas 240, 586
TURNBULL James 664; Rebecca 664
TURNER Catherine 101; Samuel 61, 470
TUTTLE Asahel 618; Lucy A. 618
TYLER Bradley William 327; Eleanor M.
  327; Harriet 443; William Bradley
  443

UMBAUGH Michael 161
UMBRAGE Joseph 574
UMPAGE Joseph 468
UPPERMAN Henry 490
URTING Charles 332; Elizabeth 332

VANDERSLOTER Rev 86
VANFOSSEN Anna 480; Edith 259
VANLEAR Matthew 107
VIERS John T. 607
VIRELY Valentine 442

WACHER Rev 417
WACHTER John 511; Michael 34, 206,
  290, 380, 386, 421; Rev 221, 255,
  343, 367
WADE Caroline Margaret Elizabeth 644;
  John 644
WAGERS Ann 318; Barbara 318; James
  191
WAGGONER Edward 604; John 203;
  Zeuriah 604
WAGNER Cresa Ann 402; Elizabeth 482
WAGONER Barbara 116; Mrs. 56, 465;
  Upton 56, 465
WALKER John 367; Josiah 1
WALLING Catharine 164
WALLMAN Jacob 588
WALSH Rev 552
WALTER John 422
WALTZ Martin 489
WALTZMAN Thomas 599
WAMPLER Ludwig 235
WARD Fanny 229
WARFIELD Charles H. 102; Surratt D.
  261
WARNER Henrietta 323
WARTTMAN John M. 406; Mathew 406
WATERS Anne Maria 102; Jacob 102;
  John T. 388; Plummer 631; William
  210, 534
WATKINS Gassaway 629

WATSON Harriet C. 414
WATTERS Rev 618
WATTS Elizabeth 613; Richard B. 613
WAUGH Beverly 529; Rev 126, 182, 261
WAYMAN Francis D. 562; Francis
  Deakins 454; Rebecca 457
WEAVER Adam 450; Casper W. 149;
  Catharine 329; James 436; Mary 567
WEBB Clarissa 664; Evan 51; George
  261; George W. 261; James 664;
  Jeremiah 261; John H. T. 261;
  Joseph B. 503; William 261, 629
WEBSTER David 523; Samuel 523, 547
WEEMS Mason I. 189
WEIGLE Margaret 86
WEISE Godfrey 90; Mrs. 90
WELLER Catherine 579;
  Henry 579; Thomas 477
WELLS Alfred 664; Elizabeth 664;
  Rebecca 664
WELTZHEIMER Dr. L. 126; Rebecca 126
WERFEL John 196
WEST Arabella 157; Benjamin 157; Dr.
  G. W. 419; Levin 584
WHAETER Rev 525
WHEELAN Martin 662
WHIFFING James 97; Sarah P. 97
WHIP George 449, 473; John 391, 531;
  Mary 449, 500; Susan 522
WHITAKER Cassandra 400; Samuel 400
WHITE Benjamin 9, 44; Rebecca 44;
  Richard 436; William 618
WHITEHEAD Emma 541; John 541
WHITEHILL James 342
WHITLER Barbara Eleanor 11
WHITMORE Jonas 571; Nicholas 212
WHITTINGDON John 468
WHITTINGTON Rebecca 326
WIDDEL Susanna 532
WIDRICK Catharine 466, 565; Elizabeth
  466
WIEST Maria M. 34
WILBURN Nancy 451
WILCOXEN Elizabeth 339
WILHELM Audolph 212
WILLET Griffith 196; Mary 196
WILLETT Burgess 655; Catherine 629;
  James 655
WILLIAMS Amanda M. 61, 470; Benjamin
  369; Elie 90; Elisha W. 620; Otho
  H. 85; William E. 85
WILLIAMSON Mr. 189

WILLIS Catharine Sarah 296; Elizabeth
  266; Henry 296; William 266
WILLSON Ann M. 407; Elizabeth Ann
  Rebecca 200; Martha 637; Richard
  A. 407; Thomas 200; William M. B.
  565, 614, 637
WILSON Charlotte Chenoweth 209;
  Henrietta 209; Martha 254; Mary
  Elizabeth Ann Rebecca 610; Thomas
  610; William M. B. 254
WINDER William H. 145, 602
WINDHAM James 624
WINEBRENER Jacob 88
WINEBRENNER Christian 126
WINN Susan B. 165
WINNULL Ann 261; Rebecca T. 545
WINPIGLER George 584; Mahala 584;
  Michael 469
WINTER Elizabeth 13; John 48, 130,
  499; Rev 218, 477; Rev J. 97, 454,
  457, 459, 462, 466, 474, 475, 482,
  483, 497; Susan 413
WIRTENBAKER William 257
WISEMAN Rev 148
WISSINGER Peter 467
WOLBERT John F. 483
WOLFE Catharine 599; Jacob 101
WOLFORD John 580
WOLGAMOT John 605
WOOD Henry 188; Mrs. 497; Sarah 188
WOODROW John 560
WOODS Nancy 23, 300; Pierce 445;
  William 23
WOOTON Martha 565
WORTHINGTON Charles C. 358; Harriett
  A. 316; Mary E. 405; Rachel 125;
  Reuben 37; Rezin H. 125; William
  316, 405
WRIGHT Benjamin 257; Henry 610; James
  548; John 507; Joseph 527; Mary
  527
WYATT Rev Dr. 165
WYLIE Sarah 101

YEAKLE Mary 178
YOKEY Henry 384
YOUNG Conrad 179; David 193, 445,
  556; Henry 404; Jacob 271; Mrs.
  507; Nicholas 37; Robert 37;
  Thomas 480, 507

INDEX

ZADWICK Rev 497
ZEALER Harriot 120; Henry 523
ZEILER George 304
ZIMMERMAN Elizabeth 366; George 366,
    481; John 261, 336, 380; Margaret
    507; Michael 481; Nicholas 227
ZOCKEY Nicholas 285; Rev 43
ZOLLICKOFFER Rev 359; Rev D. 313
ZOLLICOFFER Daniel 392
ZUCK Jacob 451

Other books by F. Edward Wright:

Abstracts of Bucks County, Pennsylvania Wills, 1685-1785

Abstracts of Cumberland County, Pennsylvania Wills, 1750-1785

Abstracts of Cumberland County, Pennsylvania Wills, 1785-1825

Abstracts of Philadelphia County Wills, 1726-1747

Abstracts of Philadelphia County Wills, 1748-1763

Abstracts of Philadelphia County Wills, 1763-1784

Abstracts of Philadelphia County Wills, 1777-1790

Abstracts of Philadelphia County Wills, 1790-1802

Abstracts of Philadelphia County Wills, 1802-1809

Abstracts of Philadelphia County Wills, 1810-1815

Abstracts of Philadelphia County Wills, 1815-1819

Abstracts of Philadelphia County Wills, 1820-1825

Abstracts of Philadelphia County, Pennsylvania Wills, 1682-1726

Abstracts of South Central Pennsylvania Newspapers, Volume 1, 1785-1790

Abstracts of South Central Pennsylvania Newspapers, Volume 3, 1796-1800

Abstracts of the Newspapers of Georgetown and the Federal City, 1789-99

Abstracts of York County, Pennsylvania Wills, 1749-1819

*Bucks County, Pennsylvania Church Records of the 17th and 18th Centuries
Volume 2: Quaker Records: Falls and Middletown Monthly Meetings*
Anna Miller Watring and F. Edward Wright

Caroline County, Maryland Marriages, Births and Deaths, 1850-1880

Citizens of the Eastern Shore of Maryland, 1659-1750

Cumberland County, Pennsylvania Church Records of the 18th Century

Delaware Newspaper Abstracts, Volume 1: 1786-1795

Early Charles County, Maryland Settlers, 1658-1745
Marlene Strawser Bates and F. Edward Wright

Early Church Records of Alexandria City and Fairfax County, Virginia
F. Edward Wright and Wesley E. Pippenger

Early Church Records of New Castle County, Delaware, Volume 1, 1701-1800

Frederick County Militia in the War of 1812
Sallie A. Mallick and F. Edward Wright

Inhabitants of Baltimore County, 1692-1763

Land Records of Sussex County, Delaware, 1769-1782

Land Records of Sussex County, Delaware, 1782-1789
Elaine Hastings Mason and F. Edward Wright

Marriage Licenses of Washington, District of Columbia, 1811-1830

*Marriages and Deaths from the Newspapers of Allegany and
Washington Counties, Maryland, 1820-1830*

Marriages and Deaths from The York Recorder, 1821-1830

*Marriages and Deaths in the Newspapers of Frederick and
Montgomery Counties, Maryland, 1820-1830*

Marriages and Deaths in the Newspapers of Lancaster County, Pennsylvania, 1821-1830

Marriages and Deaths in the Newspapers of Lancaster County, Pennsylvania, 1831-1840

Marriages and Deaths of Cumberland County, [Pennsylvania], 1821-1830

Maryland Calendar of Wills Volume 9: 1744-1749

Maryland Calendar of Wills Volume 10: 1748-1753

Maryland Calendar of Wills Volume 11: 1753-1760

Maryland Calendar of Wills Volume 12: 1759-1764

Maryland Calendar of Wills Volume 13: 1764-1767

Maryland Calendar of Wills Volume 14: 1767-1772

Maryland Calendar of Wills Volume 15: 1772-1774

Maryland Calendar of Wills Volume 16: 1774-1777

Maryland Eastern Shore Newspaper Abstracts, Volume 1: 1790-1805

Maryland Eastern Shore Newspaper Abstracts, Volume 2: 1806-1812

Maryland Eastern Shore Newspaper Abstracts, Volume 3: 1813-1818

Maryland Eastern Shore Newspaper Abstracts, Volume 4: 1819-1824

Maryland Eastern Shore Newspaper Abstracts, Volume 5: Northern Counties, 1825-1829
F. Edward Wright and Irma Harper

Maryland Eastern Shore Newspaper Abstracts, Volume 6: Southern Counties, 1825-1829

Maryland Eastern Shore Newspaper Abstracts, Volume 7: Northern Counties, 1830-1834
Irma Harper and F. Edward Wright

Maryland Eastern Shore Newspaper Abstracts, Volume 8: Southern Counties, 1830-1834

Maryland Militia in the Revolutionary War
S. Eugene Clements and F. Edward Wright

Newspaper Abstracts of Allegany and Washington Counties, 1811-1815

Newspaper Abstracts of Cecil and Harford Counties, [Maryland], 1822-1830

Newspaper Abstracts of Frederick County, [Maryland], 1816-1819

Newspaper Abstracts of Frederick County, 1811-1815

Sketches of Maryland Eastern Shoremen

Tax List of Chester County, Pennsylvania 1768

Tax List of York County, Pennsylvania 1779

Washington County Church Records of the 18th Century, 1768-1800

Western Maryland Newspaper Abstracts, Volume 1: 1786-1798

Western Maryland Newspaper Abstracts, Volume 2: 1799-1805

Western Maryland Newspaper Abstracts, Volume 3: 1806-1810

Wills of Chester County, Pennsylvania, 1766-1778

www.ingramcontent.com/pod-product-compliance
Lightning Source LLC
LaVergne TN
LVHW021537080426
835509LV00019B/2697